MW00490480

Henk Hanssen

Baby Management for Men

"Pursuing a career is only temporary.
One day you'll face the fact that
life consists of countless stages.
What, to you, is the essence of all those stages?
That's for you to finally find out,
and when you do, you could become a happy person.
But you have to be fearless."

Jo Hanssen (1925–1994)

Henk Hanssen

Baby Management for Men

a VERY practical guide

Translated and adapted from Dutch by Rogier van Bakel
Design & illustrations Erik Prinsen

pinter & martin

Baby Management for Men

First published in the the Netherlands by IkVaderBoeken 2004
This American English edition first published in Great Britain by Pinter & Martin Ltd 2013

Design and illustrations Erik Prinsen
Translated into English by Rogier van Bakel

ISBN 978-1-905177-69-1

British Library Cataloguing-in-Publication Data
A catalogue record for this book is available from the British Library.

Printed in the EU by Graficas, Spain

Pinter & Martin Ltd
6 Effra Parade
London SW2 1PS

www.pinterandmartin.com

www.babymanagement.com

Preface to the English edition

On a chilly December morning, I watched how a distinct purple line appeared on a stick. For years, the principle governing my love life had been a facsimile of my approach to work. I pursued a freelance career, both as a writer and as a lover. I believed I was unfit to be used in the classic Dutch romance recipe of two souls blending together into some sweet butter cake. With me as an ingredient, the dough would surely fail to rise. But now, there was no way back. Scared as hell, I ran to the bookstore and was glad to find *The Baby Book for Dads*. British author Peter Little offered valuable insights, such as "Never leave a baby alone outside the store or a supermarket, not even for a moment".

Insulted by this glum and self-evident advice, I hurried back to the store and came home with *A Bit Pregnant*, a book that appeared to suffer from the same hangdog undertone. A bit pregnant? I wasn't pregnant at all. Writing for men's magazines, such as *Men's Health*, I wanted to be informed in a modern, cut-the-crap, just-tell-me-the-basics sort of way. So I decided to put my annoyance to good use.

Together with a few colleagues, young fathers who had also developed an instant allergy to the average baby book, I set up a website called IkVader.nl, or iDad. Becoming or being a father is great, but let's remain men, was our key message. Want men to be involved in parenthood? Then start communicating in a way that appeals to them. Strip all the diminutives, don't spill dozens of words on baby blues and other experiences that are exclusive to moms, don't use the word parents when you only mean mothers, and, most importantly, add humor to make the baby stuff digestible. I wrote articles for the website, as well as columns in magazines – and books. I had worked as a crime reporter, a war reporter, and as a travel writer, crisscrossing Madagascar, half of Europe and Asia – and now I was writing on the art of efficient diaper changes, and fatherhood in Roman times. Before

I realized it, I had become somewhat of an expert on the subject, thanks to the lack of competition, but also because I loved the breadth, the emotional meaning, and the topicality of my subject.

Baby Management for Men was first published in 2004. Still selling in respectable numbers, the book is now the authoritative guidebook in the Netherlands for Dutch men about to become fathers. Production of the book was partly financed by the Dutch Ministry of Social Affairs. My proposal to develop a baby management workshop and book fit with their goal of lifting the barriers for men in search of information on childcare. The Ministry won't regret its investment, I guess. In 2007, a United Nations study found that Dutch children are the happiest children in the western world. (Yes, we even beat that parental paradise, Sweden, which finished as the runner-up. The U.S. and the U.K. brought up the rear.)

I admit, it would be grotesque to claim that the *Baby Management* approach is the main reason why Dutch children are reportedly so emotionally well-off. Still, there can't be too many fathers in Holland who have somehow missed the message we have been sending: becoming a father will bring about a tsunami of change in your life, so prepare yourself. Both the book and the workshop *Baby Management* created massive media attention, affirming the once-unpopular notion that a child needs a father from day one. As a measure of our success, Dutch midwives and maternity assistants now give out a brochure on *Baby Management* during their first meeting with young parents.

In all, it seems fair to say that *Baby Management* has played its role in making Dutch kids the happiest in the world. As voluminous research indicates, children develop best if they grow up in a balanced environment where both mother and father act as caregivers. And if *Baby Management* does one thing, it shows men the practice and importance of their involvement.

At this point, I wish to thank Rogier van Bakel, one of my oldest friends and father to two lovely girls, for his eloquent translation. Rogier, a Dutch-born journalist, lives in the U.S. where he has written extensively for publications such as the *New York Times* and *Rolling Stone*.

Henk Hanssen
January 2013

The Baby Manager

For tens of thousands of years, men lived like warriors, hunters, breadwinners. They dominated women and children with a superiority based on their physical strength, and they kept the economy going. However, over the last few decades – the blink of an eye in evolutionary history – men have been required to tame their hunting instincts and share their emotions. The irredeemable macho is beating a retreat on all fronts, including at home and at work. The decrees of the my-way-or-the-highway manager are now falling on deaf ears. The father who asserts his authority with a good spanking has become an object of scorn.

In today's service economy, a manager must possess both male and especially female qualities. Among those: don't bottle up emotions, put yourself in the other person's shoes, listen to your customers, gauge the fickle will of the public. "The time has come for men on the move to learn to play women's games," is how management guru Tom Peters puts it. His words clearly resonate: these days, men are eagerly acquiring soft skills left and right. They attend workshops and take classes in personal efficiency, conflict resolution, group dynamics, emotional intelligence, motivation, team-building, stress reduction, and so on.

But you'll learn the most effective new management style at your baby's crib side, and at the kitchen table. With *Baby Management* you'll kill two birds with one stone: you'll run your family like an expert, and you'll acquire the skills that will propel you ahead in today's world.

William Pollack, a Harvard psychologist, has studied the connection between the skills of being a good father and a good manager. He says: "Modern leaders, male and female, need creative vision, emotional flexibility, independent decision-making capacity, along with the ability to work within systems, creative networks and teams. They must also be able to rally support and achieve results in the midst of almost constant organizational change. My consulting experience and research have shown that, for men, those very skills are the ones most successfully learned and mastered by the well-adapted father."

In this book, the father is the consummate manager. The family is your enterprise, the mother your producer, the baby your product.

A quick clarification before we begin. To avoid switching genders from "he" to "she" and back again, I refer to the baby as a he.

Finally, I wish to thank Karen van Drongelen and Joke Hammink of the Nutrition Center, and Lydia de Raad of the Council of Cooperative Breastfeeding Organizations, for their contributions to the chapter about baby food; and Angelique Jansens, of Maternity Care Netherlands, for the expert advice on various baby care passages in the manuscript. Sincere thanks are also due to Frank Hanssen, who, both as my brother and as a professional financial planner, provided valuable insights for the chapter on financial planning; to organization adviser Peter Schoemaker and my brother Peter Hanssen for the comments and suggestions they offered to improve the personal planning chapter; to Bernadette Bergsma for her research; Lisette Roskam for compiling the index; journalist Pim Christiaans for his editorial advice; Erik Prinsen for both his art direction and his terrific illustrations; and, last but not least, my partner Ingrid van Roosmalen for her patience, and for launching and co-developing our "products", daughter Rosa and son IJsbrand.

Suggestions or other responses may be emailed to henk@babymanagement.com.

Contents

Product

1 Product

Congratulations!

Congratulations are in order on the arrival of your child. The biggest enterprise of your life is about to start! No matter how many mergers, strikes, takeovers and company insolvencies you may have survived, there is no greater challenge than launching and developing the product that is your baby. Multi-tasking, handling your time efficiently, giving entertaining presentations, controlling your budget, overcoming adversity, formulating a vision for the future – all the skills that people typically don't master until they've spent a few decades in the trenches of the business world… well, your baby is about to teach them to you, almost casually and in a very short span of time. All you need to do is become involved – and stay involved – from day one.

Four people are counting on you to pay real attention:

- **Your child** Children with involved dads simply do better in many ways than children of distant fathers. They have better motor skills, are more apt to be enterprising, and are psychologically stronger. The positive influences fathers exert on their kids are evident all the way through adolescence: girls with involved dads tend to do better in math, boys develop better problem-solving skills, and both genders are likely to be more confident and to stay away from temptations like drugs.

- **Your partner** In general, mothers tend to tax themselves heavily. One reason for that is that they think of themselves as primary caregivers, while still taking on the many responsibilities of a professional career. If she can delegate some of her tasks to you, she'll feel calmer, and your relationship is bound to improve.

• **Your employer** Almost all companies see the working world of men as entirely separate from the private sphere, the home front. The framed family photo on a manager's desk is seen as a sign of stability – rarely as a group of loved ones who may sometimes take precedence over the next business meeting. Still, a range of studies show that the conflict between home and work life is as real and as painful among working dads as it is among working moms. And it's not just hyper-ambitious yuppies who fail to strike a balance; in all socio-economic strata, fathers report a discrepancy between working hours and family time. Employers would do well to own up to that problem and to try and create a more "father-friendly" workplace. But they don't have to do this out of the goodness of their hearts. Businesses that fail to facilitate a balance between work and family will see their bottom lines affected. The disequilibrium may lead to a chain reaction of diminished concentration, more stress and sick days, et cetera. Employee retention, too, becomes an issue: people with work/home conflicts are three times as likely to change jobs. In the United States, an increasing number of companies are signing up to the belief that "better dads are better workers," thus creating father-friendly workplaces.

• **You** If you get and stay involved, fatherhood offers the ultimate opportunity for personal development, Patience, perseverance, loyalty, and responsibility are only a few of the skills you will practice (whether you like it or not!). This book is a step-by-step guide through the entire baby-management process. In 12 to-the-point chapters, we'll look at all aspects of your product, your marketing and communications strategies, your IT challenges, and the critical factors that determine the difference between profit and loss. We know you'll enjoy this book – and your baby!

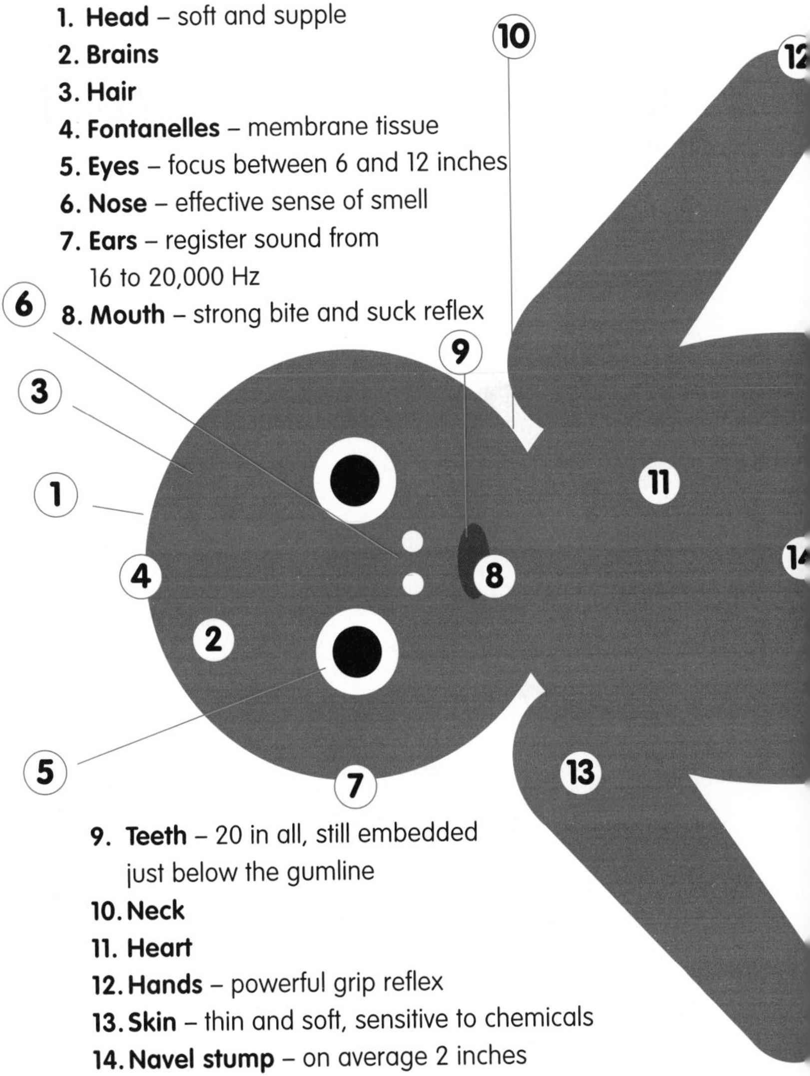

1. **Head** – soft and supple
2. **Brains**
3. **Hair**
4. **Fontanelles** – membrane tissue
5. **Eyes** – focus between 6 and 12 inches
6. **Nose** – effective sense of smell
7. **Ears** – register sound from 16 to 20,000 Hz
8. **Mouth** – strong bite and suck reflex
9. **Teeth** – 20 in all, still embedded just below the gumline
10. **Neck**
11. **Heart**
12. **Hands** – powerful grip reflex
13. **Skin** – thin and soft, sensitive to chemicals
14. **Navel stump** – on average 2 inches

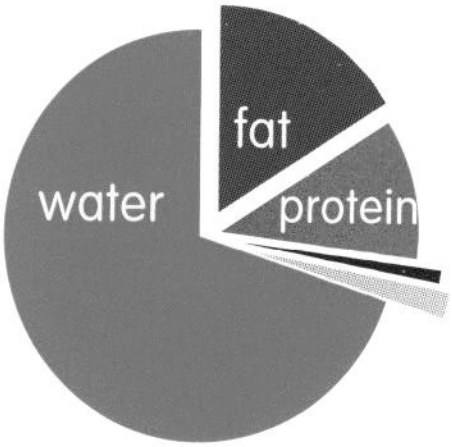

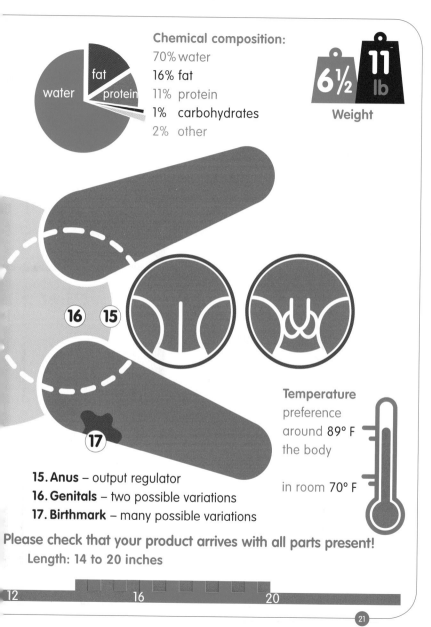

Chemical composition:

70% water
16% fat
11% protein
1% carbohydrates
2% other

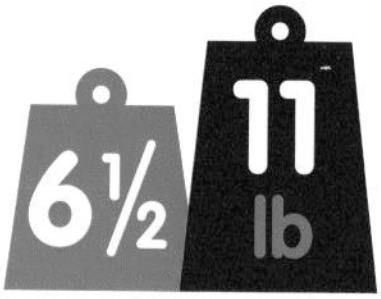

Weight

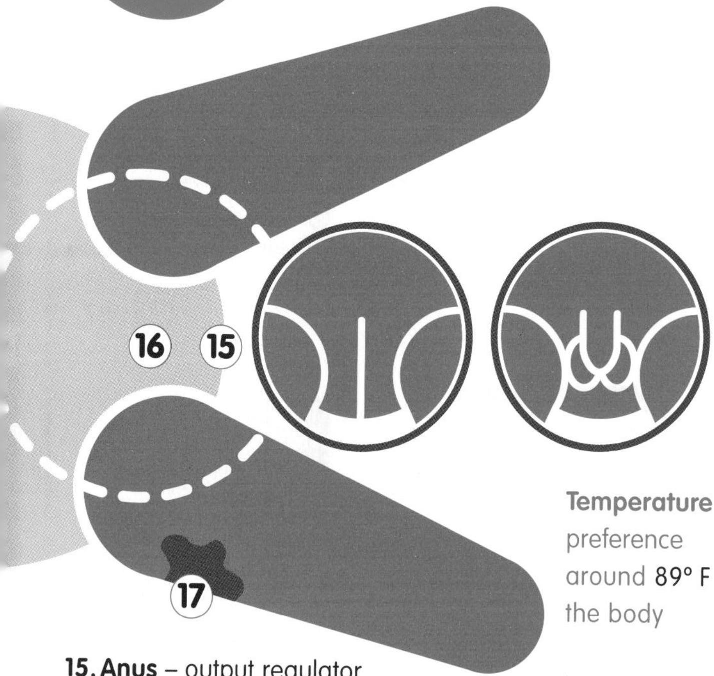

Temperature
preference
around 89° F
the body

in room 70° F

15. Anus – output regulator
16. Genitals – two possible variations
17. Birthmark – many possible variations

Please check that your product arrives with all parts present!

Length: 14 to 20 inches

Product specifications

1. Head Big: takes up a quarter of total length. The shape depends on the delivery method. Suction-cup delivery may result in temporary "conehead", gradually giving way to regular shape and proportions.
2. Brains Grow through experience. Positive impulses generate substances that create new links between brain cells.
3. Hair Not a standard accessory with each product. Downlike hair may appear on shoulders and back (or, rarely, over the entire body); this disappears in a few weeks.
4. Fontanelles To enable the baby's passage through the birth canal, its head is momentarily compressed. This ingenious feature exists thanks to supple membranes (fontanelles) that connect the bones of the cranium. The fontanelles on the top of the baby's head are the softest spot of these membranes. The word is derived from Latin and means "little fountain", as fontanelles were at one time thought to produce fluids. During the first two months the membranes grow because the skull itself grows, but the skull parts gradually converge and the seams between them tighten up, eliminating the soft spots.
5. Eyes After delivery, the eyes stare at the mother's face for a good hour, especially keen on detecting movement. Big pupils draw people's attention. Eye color (like skin and hair color) is determined by natural levels of the pigment melanine. Caucasian (white) babies are usually outfitted with blue or grey eyes, while most African American and Asian newborns have brown eyes. The final color is evident after about a year, during which pigment may increase.
6. Nose Quintessential organ whose primary function is finding food. After a few days, the nose can distinguish between mother's own milk and that of other producers.

7. Ears Sensitive to volume and pitch. Attempt language acquisition skills from day one. Most receptive to high-pitched human voices.

8. Mouth Built-in alarm function. Produces smiles after four weeks. Tastebuds prefer sweet foods.

9. Teeth There is a 0.2 per cent chance that your product comes equipped with one visible tooth. Caesar and Napoleon belonged to this select group.

10. Neck Muscles not yet developed.

11. Heart Weighs 30 grams (1 ounce); has a rate of 140 beats per minute.

12. Hands During its first days on earth your baby is capable of firmly grasping the hand or finger of another human. This reflex loses strength as time goes by.

13. Skin Your baby is delivered in white-gray packaging of fatty sebaceous matter and skin flakes. The most important function of this greasy layer is facilitating the baby's exit through the birth canal, but it may also protect against early infections. The fatty layer recedes into the skin naturally, necessitating no intervention, but in the U.S. the baby is still usually washed after delivery.

14. Navel stump The umbilical cord is literally the lifeline through which your producer provides your product with oxygen and nourishment. After the baby's birth, this vital cord keeps pulsating for about five minutes. As soon as it stops, the umbilical cord is cut and clamped. The remaining stump dries and turns black, and eventually falls off after 5 to 10 days. Until then, it must be kept clean and dry.

15. Anus Equipped with 2 functions: waste management, and as a repository for a thermometer.

16. Genitals Still comparatively large. Body will grow faster than sex organs.

17. Birthmark Your product may sport a birthmark varying in size and severity. Consult your midwife or physician.

The APGAR score

In the minutes after the birth, the midwife or doctor will check your baby's vital signs twice: once immediately after the child is born, and again 5 minutes later. This "life function" test is based on a model developed in 1952 by New York anaesthesiology professor Virginia Apgar. She considered birth as "the riskiest moment in a person's life", and devised a test that indicates the possible presence of a medical emergency.

The Apgar test is not just named after its inventor; it's also an acronym that stands for appearance (color), pulse (heart rate), grimace (response to stimuli), activity (healthy muscle movement), and respiratory effort (breathing). Your child may score anywhere from 1 to 10, with a maximum of two points per category.

Here's the test presented in a table:

APGAR score	0 points	1 point	2 points
Body color	Blue	Body pink, limbs blue	Pink all over
Heart rate	Undetectable	Under 100 bpm	Over 100 bpm
Stimulus response	None	Grimaces	Sneezes!
Muscle moves/ tension	Very low	Low	High
Breathing	None	Slow, irregular	Cries

Results

The results indicate how the baby has braved the birth and how well he is adjusting. The numbers carry the following interpretation:

< 2 points

Your baby is struggling to the point of a medical emergency, especially if the second test shows little or no improvement.

3–4 points

A difficult start. The second test should turn out better.

5–6 points

Often a normal score during the first test. Your baby has trouble with the enormous change of environment and may need help in the form of extra oxygen. No cause for undue alarm, as long as the second test shows a score of seven points or better.

7–8 points

A fine score. You've got a healthy kid.

9–10 points

It doesn't get better than this. Your baby has lust for life, and then some!

Remember, though, that the rule of thumb is to not worry too much if the score is below par. There is no more hectic moment in a person's life than birth. Most children who experience some difficulty during this stage recover quickly without lasting harmful effects.

2

Planning

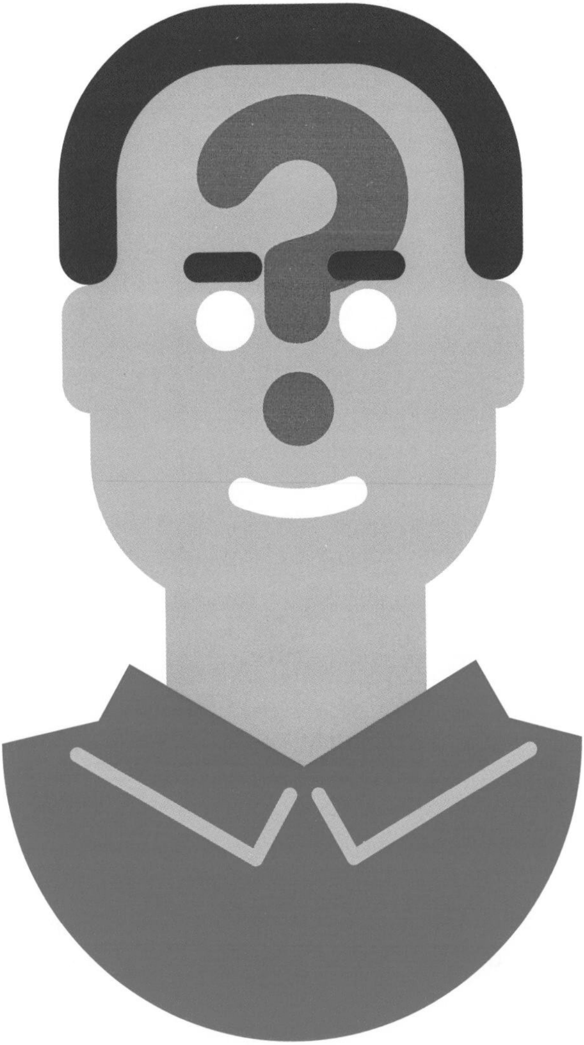

Personal planning

You can find a course, a seminar, or a business guru for virtually every branch of management – except baby management. And yet, solid preparation is key. Read on.

Vanished rituals

Becoming a father is bound to be the biggest change of your life. It affects every aspect of you – emotional, financial, physical, and spiritual. For women this is pretty much old hat, business as usual; their bodies flow from low to high tide every month, they experience swelling bellies and other changes during pregnancy, and menopause ushers in yet another transformation. For men, changes come more suddenly, almost unexpectedly. Apart from thinning hair and some thickness around the waist, their bodies have no innate signal functions. In a society where rituals have as good as vanished, changes in a man's life are typically brought about by external factors: marriage, losing a job, divorce, moving into a new home, and birth. Often, the true significance of the change doesn't hit home until after the event, sometimes precipitating a shock – the rare if classic example being the new dad who skips town and becomes a deadbeat soon after the birth.

Personal Fatherhood Plan

In the next section we invite you to develop a plan – the Personal Fatherhood Plan. How prepared are you to be a dad? What's your motivation for having kids? Which circumstances determine your success? What is your fatherhood philosophy? And how will you implement it all?

Create a Personal Fatherhood Plan

The 7 Father Questions

Get out a pen and a piece of paper and answer the following questions. Your responses will provide an insight into what made you want to be a father:

1. Why do you want to be a dad? Was it an "accident"? A considered choice? The wish of your partner?

2. How would you like to be remembered as a dad? Fifty years from now, your children will want to put some fitting words on your gravestone. What will they decide upon?

3. Which characteristics of your own father and mother would you like to pass on to your child? Why?

4. Which characteristics of your own father and mother *don't* you want to pass on? Why?

5. Have you come to a clear, detailed agreement with your partner about who'll take care of the child?

6. Will you take paternity leave? Have you made arrangements with your employer?

7. What do you see as the primary personal dilemmas concerning your impending fatherhood?

The 7 Dimensions of Effective Fatherhood

Now that you've gained a better understanding of your internal motivation, let's look at external factors. Research shows that the quality of fatherhood is determined by seven "dimensions". In this section we provide brief explanations of each one. Reach for that pen and sheet of paper again. Honestly judge every aspect by giving it a score from 1 to 10. On page 33 you'll find a way to calculate the quality of these external factors.

1. Your partner's attitude

It goes without saying that everything begins with your partner: the child is born in a literal symbiosis with the mother. She more or less controls the "keys" to fatherhood. In a way, she must enable you to step up to the plate. Will she let you thrive in your new role, or will she hog all the crucial childcare activities and shower you in criticism? Write down a number for the degree to which she is likely to let you achieve your fatherhood potential.

2. Flexible hours

Seventy per cent of all men have trouble combining work and home. It's often their hours that prevent them from being a fully-fledged partner in raising a child. Award a score to reflect how flexible your hours are.

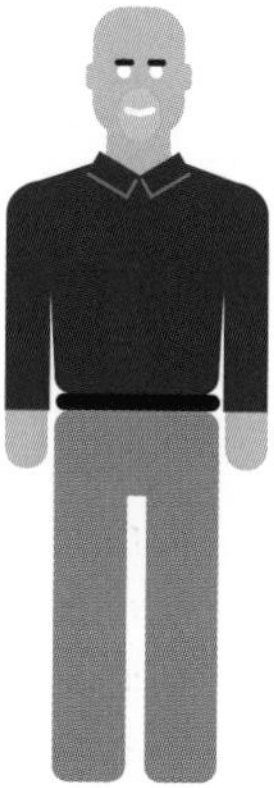

3. Example set by your own father

The broad lines of parental behavior are biologically determined; the details, however, are slowly acquired knowledge. Your style as a father can't help but be greatly influenced by your experiences with your own parents. What kind of example did your dad set? Award a score for the inspiration he is to you.

4. Extracurricular activities

Whether you like it or not, your child will wreak havoc on your social life. Are your non-working hours planned and spoken for? Indicate with a number how flexible your extracurricular time is.

5. Support system

Do the soon-to-be grandparents live just down the block? How many neighbors and friends with children live within a mile or so? The degree to which your social circle can be counted on to help with childcare in a pinch is a factor in how flexible you can be. Judge the quality and quantity of your support system by awarding it a number.

6. Opinions on men and baby care

Does the prospect of changing diapers or pushing a stroller fill you with dread? Your outlook on what it means to do "manly" things helps determine how involved and successful you will be as a dad. Give a number that reflects your opinion of how interchangeable men's and women's childcare tasks really are.

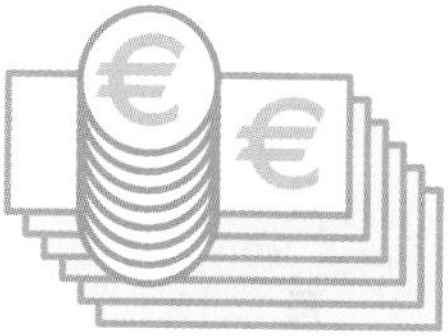

7. Satisfaction with finances

After the birth of their first child, many men work more instead of less – it's probably a primary instinct that kicks in and commands men to gather firewood and hunt for meat. It's an understandable reaction, because raising children is a pricey proposition. How are you doing financially? If you're dissatisfied with your money situation and are likely to work harder as a result, you'll have less time to spend with the kids. Write down a number that expresses how happy you are with your current financial position.

How effective can you be?

Multiply your average score by 1.43, and see to what degree the external factors enable your effectiveness as a father.

Dimension	Score
1. **Partner's attitude**	....
2. **Flexible hours**	....
3. **Example set by your own father**	....
4. **Extracurricular activities**	....
5. **Support system**	....
6. **Opinions on men and baby care**	....
7. **Satisfaction with finances**	....
Total score	________
Average	....
Your effectiveness (total score x 1.43)	% ....

My Fatherhood Vision

The secret of any successful manager lies in his ability to convince others of his vision, his mission statement, his mantra. If you have this talent, banks will provide that loan that previously hung by a thread, employees will agree to forgo a raise, and the tax auditor will allow several of your more creative business deductions. Provided it is well thought-out and seductively presented, a real vision can flatten previously insurmountable problems. You'll need the same capability as a baby manager. After all, you're embarking on a new life as a team – and any team, no matter how small, needs a common goal.

Take another look at your answers to the 7 Father Questions. Reread how you assessed yourself relative to the 7 Dimensions. Now try to capture in words what kind of a father you will be. Just answer these two questions:

1. My personal ambition as a father is:

....

....

....

2. This is how I'll realize my ambition:

....

....

....

....

Your Personal Fatherhood Plan is now complete. Take a look at how your vision relates to your inner motivation and the external factors. What are your strong points, and where might there be room for improvement?

Legal planning

Make sure that, even before your product is launched, your legal position is rock solid. Lawyers are a poor substitute for planning.

Custody

I don't mean primarily the kind of custody that is awarded in a divorce proceeding. Having custody of a child simply means that you are legally obligated to care for and raise the child until adulthood. Also, you are the legal representative of the child, and share legal responsibility for his actions.

Pater familias

It was pretty simple in Roman times. A newborn or adopted child was placed at the feet of the father. If he didn't pick it up, the child was banned from the household; if he did, he accepted it as a member of his *familia*. The *familia* was a tight legal unit that thrived on discipline, subjugation, and obedience. The father, a.k.a. the *pater familias*, ruled over his wives, his offspring, and his slaves. Being a father meant that the law bestowed generous rights upon him that, taken together, were called *patria potestas*.

Fallen apart

The old Roman notion of the all-powerful father, whose authority even superseded that of mere man-made laws, has fallen apart. These days, family law allows for a dozen different *kinds* of fathers, including the biological father, the stepfather, the adoptive father, the step-adoptive father, the anonymous sperm donor, and the father whose frozen sperm was used to conceive after his death. Though laws vary by country, each type of father tends to have different rights and obligations.

Do dads still lay down the law?

The father of yore, with all his rights, is today's mother. In most western cultures, if she's of age and unmarried, custody of the child is automatically hers. The father who wants shared custody needs her permission, or the intervention of a court. Married parents who divorce may get joint custody, but if the mother petitions the court for sole custody and wins, the father typically has to keep paying for the child's upbringing, even though he may not be allowed even to visit.

If the marriage does come apart at the seams, children may be subject to one of two kinds of custody: with and without paternal care. Even in our times of widespread gender equality, mothers claim and receive custody of the kids in the vast majority of cases. Most of these kids lose regular contact with their biological fathers. Although statistics vary from country to country, these numbers apply to the entire western world: 9 out of 10 fathers leave the house after a divorce. Joint custody is the outcome in only 2 out of 10 divorce cases. In 7 out of 10 divorces, the father is declared the non-custodial parent. About half of divorced dads see their children once a week. The older the children, though, the more divorced fathers are involved in their care. Still, only 6 per cent of children under 7 live with their divorced dads.

Children who live with their mothers tend to experience weakening bonds with their fathers. Fourteen per cent of these kids never see their father; 26 per cent see him fewer than once a week; 60 per cent see him once a week. Almost half never spend the night at their father's place. So, for an ever-increasing number of children in the developed world, the father isn't even a vague figure who plays a supporting role in the family scenario. He has become a memory, deleted from the script altogether. In America's inner cities, the traditional family has disappeared almost completely. Fewer than

1 in 10 children in these neighborhoods has a live-in father. Many fathers and a sizeable number of mothers deplore the inequality of the situation. On the other hand, there is a large group of moms seeking to maintain the limited contact between dads and offspring. Fathers who were relatively involved in the children's upbringing tend to stay that way even after a divorce.

Parental plan

Most western cultures are trapped in a motherhood ideology, as Louis Tavecchio, an Amsterdam University childcare professor, puts it. Since the beginning of the 20th century, motherly care has been romanticized, feeding the notion that childcare was the woman's exclusive right. From time to time, politicians have tried to balance parental care by including the father, but feminism and the women's movement, which consider the paternal family the cradle of male chauvinist suppression, succeeded in preventing changes to the law. Nevertheless, there are signs of change. In a few European countries, "parental plans" are obligatory for couples who wish to divorce. In this official document, they must agree on custody-sharing after the break-up, even detailing things such as clothing styles, allowance, curfews, sleepovers, haircut frequency, and so on.

Mediators are available to help parents devise such a plan. Every divorce or registered-partnership dissolution petition should include a parental plan. The judge only agrees to the divorce if he thinks the plan passes muster. Norman Mailer once mused, "You never know your wife until you meet her in court." Under all circumstances, try to avoid putting his sentiment to the test by drawing up a parental plan when your relationship is smooth as silk, even if it's not mandatory in your country.

How do you get legal custody?

Being the biological father gives you about the same legal status as a sperm donor. How do you get a real say?

You are married

If you're married there's no fuss: you'll automatically receive legal custody of your child. If you're in an officially registered (domestic) partnership, check for state-specific regulations.

You are not married

If you're not married, or are living alone, or you live together without the benefit of a registered partnership, you'll need a legal procedure to be recognized as the father. Because there is usually no question about who the mother is (since she gave birth to the child), she starts out automatically with sole physical and legal custody. Even if you've lived with your child's mother for a decade, in most countries you need an official document that enumerates the duties, obligations, and rights that you have regarding the upkeep of your new addition. Basically, once you have this paper, you are a parent in the eyes of the law. Without the Acknowledgment of Paternity (AOP), as it is called in many U.S. states, or the Parental Responsibility Agreement as it's known in the U.K., you have no say whatsoever – not in the surname, not in medical matters pertaining to your child, and not in overseas travel. Your opinion won't even count if your partner wants to give the child up for adoption. You and your partner must both sign the document.

You can (and should) prepare the document during her pregnancy, or as soon as possible after birth. If not, the only right

you might end up with is the right to pay child support for offspring you may not even be allowed to see. Unmarried Britons are lucky: having the father's name on the birth certificate bestows parental responsibility.

Registration

One of the few remaining tasks that falls exclusively to the father is taking care of the baby's registration. In the United States, the hospital usually takes care of the paperwork. In most European countries, you need to appear in person at the town hall; or, in the UK, at a registry office. The moment your child's life "officially" starts still holds something magical. Bring a friend with a video camera!

In the U.S., you'll need a birth certificate form. It's available at any courthouse in the state in which your child was born, but in the interest of simplicity, it's usually provided by the hospital. You'll need to submit the following information:

- Child's full name
- Date of birth
- Sex
- City and county of birth
- Hospital or other location where the birth occurred
- Maiden name of mother
- Your full name

Not required but recommended: apply for your new baby's social security number at the same time. If you're not married, bring your Acknowledgement of Paternity document; without it, your name won't appear on the birth certificate.

In the case of an unassisted childbirth or a home birth, there is some extra paperwork to go through before you receive the birth certificate. Don't wait too long with filling out the forms. In the Netherlands you risk a stiff fine if you register your baby later than three working days, so it's wise to check the deadline.

Baby management at work

Baby management can be more demanding than many a regular management job. Paradoxically, though, you're just going to have to do it in your spare time – well, during your non-career hours, anyway. Striking a balance between your work and home life is one of the greatest challenges you'll face.

Today's dads

For almost 10 years, I have been giving workshops for those about to become fathers. Over the course of an evening, the participants are challenged to ask themselves what becoming a dad means to them and how they'll cope with it. No, they're not tie-dye-wearing softies. They're entrepreneurs, marketing managers, and freelancers who want to resolve the potential conflict between the two most important parts of their lives: being there for their families *and* succeeding in their careers. That pivotal question – how to combine work and family life – is, of course, a recurring one during each workshop. Sure, the role of the breadwinner is still crucial to participants' identities as men and fathers. But these dads, like so many other present-day fathers, want more than financial responsibility: they want to be involved in the lives of their children.

Work/home conflict the same

When asked what is most important in their lives, kids or career, 70 per cent of all men choose their offspring. At the same time though, many fathers report that they can't find enough time to be with their kids. Copious research shows that men and women experience virtually the same level of conflict between work and home (40 per cent of

men, 37 per cent of women). And those numbers don't just apply to upper-middle class partners who both work. Fathers from all socioeconomic strata report, reluctantly and with regret, that they don't spend enough hours with their children. Whether their spouses work full-time, part-time, or not at all, has no bearing on this finding. Of all the men from traditional families – in which the woman is a homemaker – 40 per cent confess to feeling "some friction between home and work", and 16 per cent report "lots of tension".

Work/life balancing

Experiencing difficulties when combining life at work and at home is a formidable stress factor. Worries about a sick child at home, or feelings of guilt because you can't spend as much time with your offspring as you'd like, can lead to a chain reaction of reduced concentration, sick days, even the desire to change jobs.

Employees with work/life conflicts are three times as likely to look for work elsewhere. More and more employers recognize the importance of work/life balancing. But the measures they take to resolve the imbalance are either designed for all employees, or specifically for women. The expectation is that men will let their children take a backseat to their careers, whereas it's the reverse for women. For many women, maternity leave is a stepping stone to part-time work, not least because most men don't discuss their own time conflicts, or attempt to camouflage them.

Father-friendly policies

Some companies, in Europe, Australia and the U.S., are trying to fix the imbalance. Believing that "better dads make better workers", these businesses implement father-friendly programs. Anecdotal reports suggest the programs are highly successful. The companies find that expenditures for their father-friendly approach are more than offset by higher productivity, and by savings on both medical benefits and recruiting costs (the latter, of course, become inevitable when an employee with children leaves for the greener pastures of a parent-friendly competitor). But what do these father-friendly policies entail?

Invisible dilemma

A father-friendly company is an organization where everyone, whether they toil in the boardroom or the mailroom, is wholly convinced that it's good business to allow men to be involved fathers. The implementation of father-friendly policies means identifying and facing the "invisible dilemma". It starts with an anonymous intra-company poll among all male employees (or a representative sample); questions and answers are geared toward discovering whether male workers experience a severe disconnect between home life and work life. Based on the results, a number of initiatives can be discussed, such as:

- **More flexible work hours** – Employees won't work less, but gain a measure of control over *when* they work.
- **"Father-friendly" internal communications** – Does the company "speak" in a manner that appeals to dads?
- **Management commitment** – Not just words – actions.
- **Father-friendly childcare** – Are fathers being involved in childcare enrollment, PTA meetings and other parent events? Are company letters about childcare addressed to mothers *and* fathers?
- **Elaborate (company-specific) information exchange** about fatherhood on the company's intranet – not just aimed at young dads, but also at fathers who may be divorcing.
- **Promoting involvement in education**
- **Paternity leaves squared** – A leave of absence may be granted not just around the baby's birth, but also when the child falls ill.
- **Paid parental leaves**
- **Employer-sponsored college savings plans**
- **Workshops and seminars**

A distant dream? Bear in mind that there are companies that even inform fathers of the advantages of breastfeeding, based on the knowledge that breastfed babies are generally healthier and that their parents don't miss as much work.

Your role in making it happen

You could wait for your company to introduce father-friendly policies. On the other hand, you could also take a modest first step yourself. Eastman Kodak, the imaging products company based in Rochester, New York, became a leader of the work-life-balance movement in the wake of a 1991 initiative by a dozen employees who wanted to gauge the interest of co-workers in a parenting group. The 12 received thousands of responses, which led to the "Working Parents League", an organization that looks out for the interests of employees with kids.

Requesting flexible hours

It's all well and good to conclude you need more control over scheduling your work hours, but how do you convince your boss?

- Don't present your request as if you're asking for a favor. Stress that it's a business proposal that's advantageous to both parties.
- Discuss your request with your co-workers in advance, and make sure they're on board with it.
- Make your tasks and results as measurable as possible, and clarify how the quantity and quality of your work can be controlled.
- Never imply that your continued loyalty to the company is at stake. But don't let your boss play the loyalty card either.
- Propose a trial period.

Carefully prepare your proposal for more flexible work hours, using the example on the next page as a starting point.

Proposal for flexible hours (concept)

Name: ....
Date: ....
Job title: ....
Department: ....

Requests : O part-time work O 4-day working week of … hrs a day
O telecommuting O other, as follows............

Reason for proposal: ....

New arrangement valid as of: ....

New work hours:
Current working week: Total of .... hours
Sun: Mon: Tue: Wed: Thu: Fri: Sat:

Future work week: Total of .... hours
Sun: Mon: Tue: Wed: Thu: Fri: Sat:

My new working week has the following consequences for:

- Colleagues / team members: ....

Possible solution: ....

- Customers: ....

Possible solution: ....

- Others: ....

Possible solution: ....

My new work week will save the company money, as follows:
Travel expenses/lodging: ....
Other: ....

With my new work week, the company will incur additional costs:

....

The results of my new work week will be measured as follows:

....

I propose a work evaluation on or after:

....

The paternity leave benefit

Unless you're a Swede, you probably have to pay for your own paternity leave – if you are allowed to take paternity leave at all, that is.

Scandinavian paradise

Living in Sweden means barren winters, beer that costs a fortune, and getting taxed almost beyond compare. But, as soon as you become a father, you do get something in return: oceans of time to bond with your child. Currently, Sweden grants fathers the right to 2 months of leave, paid at up to 80 per cent of their salary. The leave may be taken any time from birth until the child starts school. Additionally, couples have 9 nicely compensated months of leave to divide between themselves as they see fit. Norwegian and Icelandic men get similarly generous arrangements, but the rest of the world's dads probably have to pay for their own leave – or get by with no leave at all.

Daddy Track

In the Netherlands, fathers aren't pampered by the government as much as you might think. There's a 2-day fully paid paternity leave right after birth; just enough to get your child registered and have a baby shower. Corporate employees have the right to take unpaid leave of up to 26 weeks that confers a small tax break. One reason for the reluctance to offer a more generous arrangement is the idea that men won't take advantage of paternity leave, even when it's offered to them. However, research shows men are willing to switch to the "daddy track" for a while, if their job is secure and their colleagues are supportive. As long as fatherhood is regarded as an obstacle instead of an asset to your career, paternity leave

– in other words, the chance to give your fatherhood a head start – won't gain much popularity.

More kids, more money

That fatherhood is an asset was shown recently by German researchers who studied the effect of having children on the salary of men. Result? The more kids you have, the higher your income! You could consider extending your family to biblical proportions, because each child leads to a salary increase of three per cent. The effect is especially pronounced among higher-educated men. Why? The researchers point to a couple of reasons. Fathers put in more hours at work and they plan their careers meticulously – something that their employers like to reward. Other studies indicate that fatherhood equips men with skills that propel them higher up the career ladder.

Management training

So companies and their employees have solid business reasons to implement paternity leave and other measures to encourage men to become (and stay) involved fathers. Fatherhood could even function as a framework for management training. A couple of years ago I mentioned this idea to the CEO of a large European insurance company. He had his own personal reasons for agreeing to my suggestion: "My daughter is going to college this autumn. She's leaving and I have the feeling I don't really know who she is. I don't want my people to go through the same." We set up a try-out workshop called "fatherhood as management training".

The 1-day event was attended by 14 top-level managers who were asked to chart the differences in the ways they were perceived by their subordinates and by their children. Our goal was to show that the private and corporate worlds aren't as separate as they might seem – in fact, kitchen-table strategies could be put to work at the office. "My two adolescents taught me how to deal with a self-centered colleague," one of the managers said.

Unforeseen adversaries

Although the participants were unanimously positive about the try-out, further development of the course was torpedoed from an unsuspected corner. Female managers couldn't agree to the implicit message of the initiative. "Why is fatherhood suddenly regarded as an asset to men's careers when having kids is seen as a burden on our development?" they argued successfully. It seems paternity leave not only needs corporate support, but also motherly approval.

Mainte

nance

3

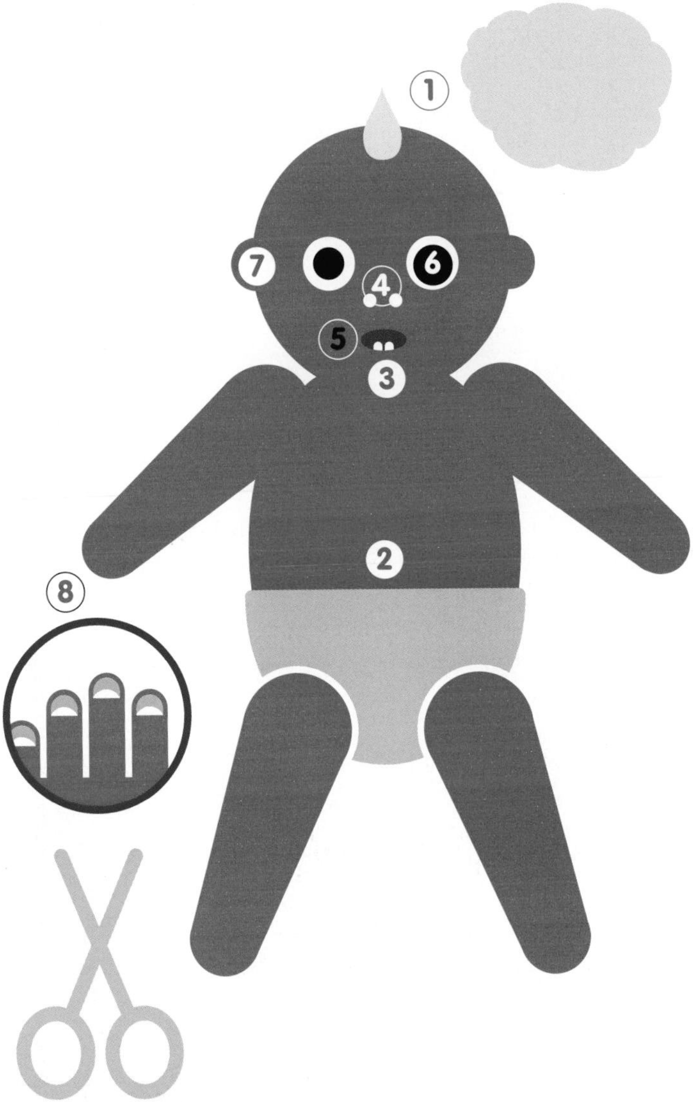
1
7
6
4
5
3
2
8

Maintenance

1. Head Support it gently and wash with warm water without exerting much pressure with your palms or fingers. Remember the fontanelles. Pat dry. If the scalp is flaky or crusty, your child probably has cradle cap, which is common and no cause for worry. Don't wash the affected area with water and soap; use cotton wool and baby oil instead. The crusts will soften and detach. At that point, soap and water may be applied to the area. If the phenomenon returns, see a doctor.
2. Navel stump This protuberance will dry out and fall off. You can bathe the baby, navel stump and all, provided that you gently dry the area afterwards. Use a cotton swab dipped in alcohol. A pediatrician or other maternity specialist can help if you have questions.
3. Teeth Gently rub with a damp cloth. When the teeth become bigger and more numerous, use a soft brush.
4. Nose Equipped with a self-cleaning mechanism. Tiny hairs on the mucous membrane push dust and slime to the nasal opening. Sneezing usually expels it altogether. Maintain nostrils with the corner of a washcloth.
5. Mouth Self-cleaning.
6. Eyes Tear ducts take care of cleaning – fully automated process!
7. Ears Use the wet corner of a towel or washcloth to clean only the ear's exterior parts. The ear canal does not need to be cleaned; earwax transports dirt outward, aided by the ear canal's tiny hairs.
8. Nails To prevent scratching, nails must be trimmed regularly. Use clean nail clippers, preferably swabbed with alcohol, or blunt-ended baby scissors. If the baby objects, cut his nails while he's sleeping.

Cleaning

To keep your product functioning efficiently, it has to be cleaned thoroughly every two or three days. Make sure the room is nice and warm. Take off your watch, wash your hands, and keep the following items at the ready. Don't forget anything – you can't walk away from the baby to retrieve a forgotten item!

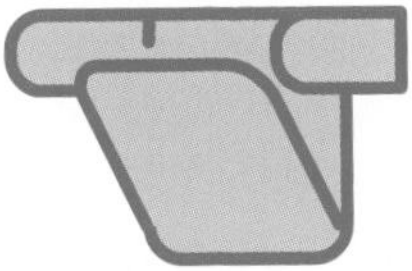

- Dry cotton towels
- Clean clothes
- Clean diaper
- Baby soap or shampoo (use sparingly, just water is usually fine)
- Wash cloth or bath sponge
- Baby powder or baby oil
- Cotton wool or cotton swabs
- Two bowls
- Rubber mat
- Thermometer

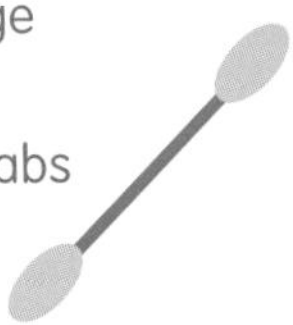

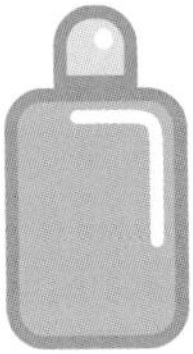

Mat

Use two bowls of warmish water, one with soap (if you wish) and one without. Cover one side of the baby's body with a towel while you work on the other with soap and water.

Rinse off with normal water. Dry well, especially in hard-to-reach skin folds. If desired, use baby (not talcum) powder, or baby oil.

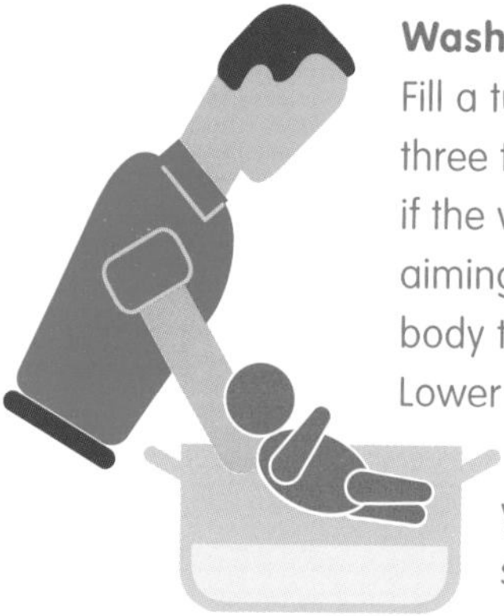

Wash basin

Fill a tub or basin with water up to a depth of three to four inches. Use an elbow to determine if the water temperature is all right: you're aiming for about 98.5 degrees Fahrenheit – body temperature. Warm is good, hot is not. Lower the baby backside down. Wash, rinse, and dry. Hold the baby's left arm with your left hand, and simultaneously support his head with your left arm.

Bath

Put a rubber anti-slip mat in the tub (you can also use a basin on a sturdy stand). Wrap a towel around protruding faucets and other hot bath fixtures which could hurt the child. Fill the tub or basin with a quantity of water, paying attention to the temperature. Carefully lower the baby. Sometimes it helps him enjoy the experience if you buy a small inflatable mattress that you can use in the tub; put the child down on it and gently rock him.

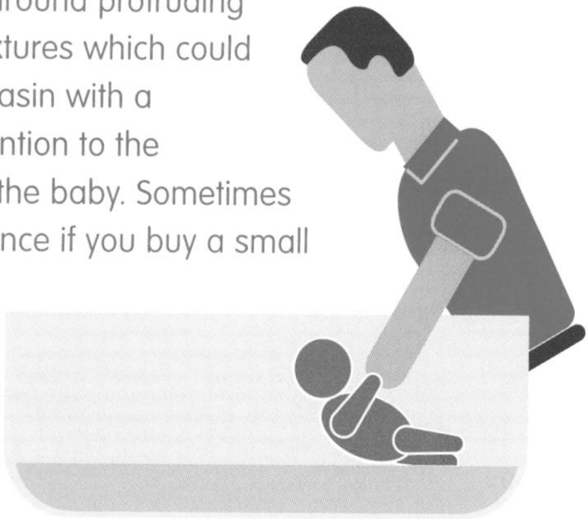

!

- Never leave a baby alone during a bath. One to two inches of water are enough for an infant to drown in!
- Always bathe a baby before his meal; afterwards, he wants to sleep.
- Face, buttocks, and genitals ought to be cleaned several times a day.

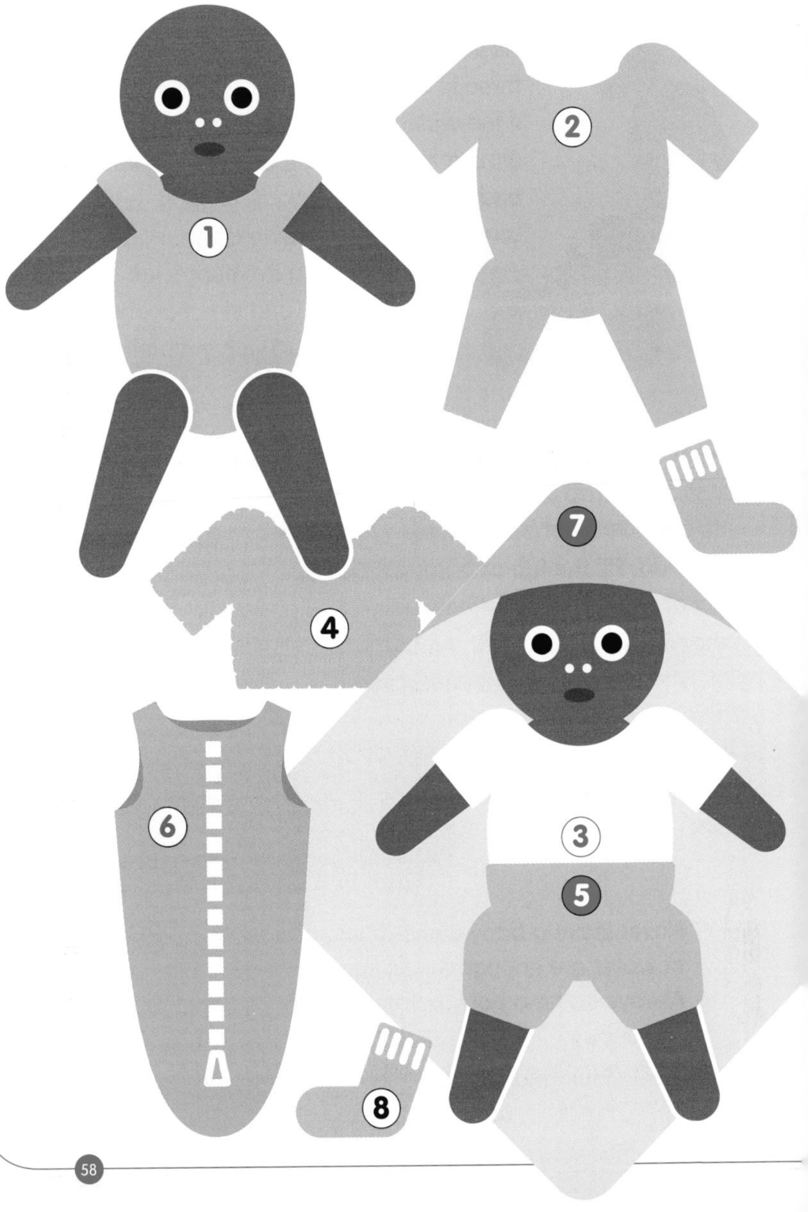
1
2
7
4
6
3
5
8

Packaging

After the delivery, your product won't be able to regulate his own temperature. You'll have to help with packaging that allows him to keep his body temperature around 98.5 degrees Fahrenheit (37 degrees Celsius). The packaging can double as protection.

1. Onesie Basic packaging. The first layer of clothing. Available in regular cotton or terry cotton, with long or short sleeves, with buttons, snaps, etc. You'll need six or more of these. 2. Jumpsuit A sort of mini-coverall, usually with feet, also available in cotton or terry cotton. Minimum number needed: three. 3. T-shirt Usually cotton, long- or short-sleeved. Get at least six of these. 4. Sweater or cardigan Get some with a wide neck opening or with shoulder fasteners. Wool or synthetic. Three should do it. 5. Diaper pants Pants with short legs. Not strictly necessary, but convenient during the summer. 6. Wearable sleeping bag Comes with a zipper, can be sleeveless. Get three of these. 7. Receiving blanket Handy when the baby needs to be kept warm in a pinch. In the summer time, choose flannel or cotton; in the cold months, wool. 8. Socks When he begins to crawl, keep his feet warm with cotton or wool socks. You'll need eight pairs, for starters.

!

- Close a zipper at a safe distance from the skin.
- Don't bundle and overheat your baby. He'll be most comfortable at a room temperature of about 73 degrees Fahrenheit (23 degrees Celsius).
- Pick clothes that are easy to get on and off.
- Pay attention to your detergent. Chemicals can trigger skin irritations and allergies. Look for hypoallergenic alternatives if this is an issue.

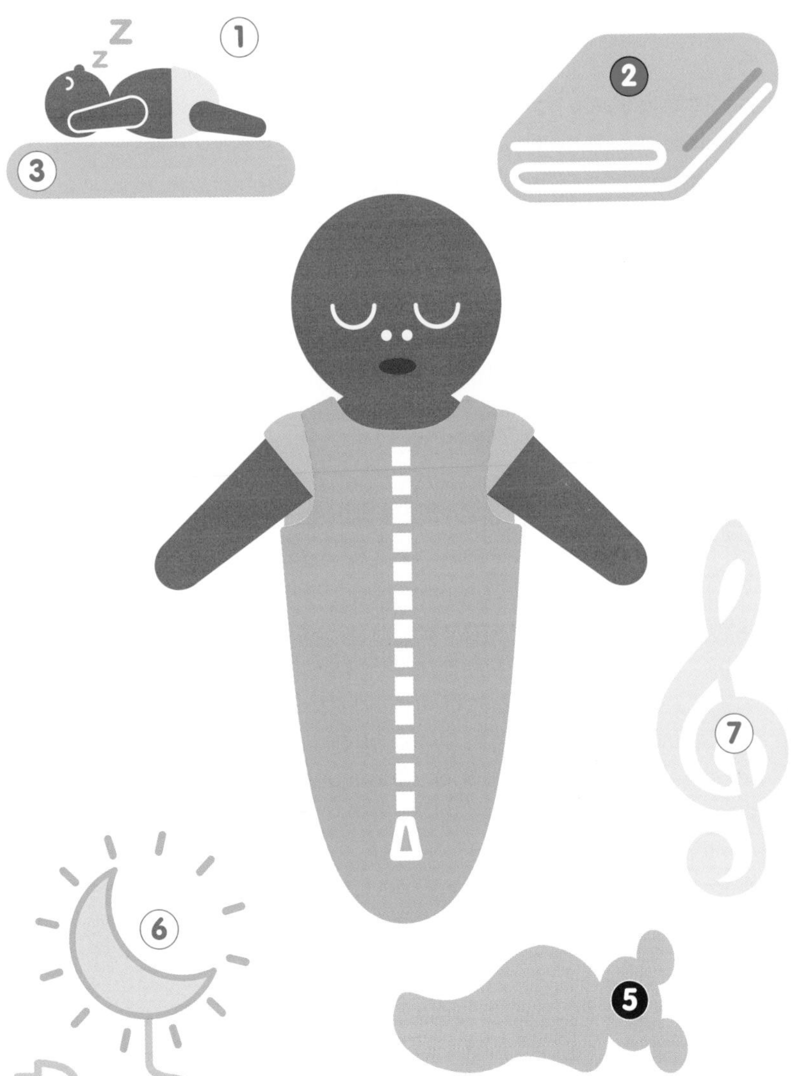

Z
z
1
2
3
7
6
5

Charging

Your product's energy is generated by sleep. See to it that sleeping is a natural and undisturbed process. Follow these tips and guidelines:

1. Sleep orientation Wherever the baby sleeps, put him on his back, not on his tummy. Main reason: back slumberers have a lower incidence of "crib death." Sudden Infant Death Syndrome (SIDS), a.k.a. crib death, is a catch-all name for the phenomenon of babies being found lifeless in their cribs. SIDS is the leading cause of death for infants between one month and one year of age. Most of these infants are between two and four months old. Preemies and low-weight babies are also at risk, and SIDS strikes boys more often than girls – no one knows why. Babies who sleep with a pacifier have a lower incidence of SIDS, possibly because they feel more comfortable and, as a rule, don't toss and turn as much. But pacifiers are not without disadvantages. Wait until breastfeeding is established before using one. The jury is still out on what causes SIDS. If your child is deemed to have a higher-than-usual risk of SIDS, his sleeping behavior will become the subject of medical scrutiny. Possible solutions are a device that monitors the baby's breathing, or special pajamas (see chapter 10).
2. Blankets Don't use a single quilt or comforter but one or two light cotton blankets. Tuck in the blankets at the foot and the sides of the mattress so that the baby can't kick them loose and pull them over his face. For a new baby, "shorten" the bed, by tucking the bedding into a roll closer to the baby's feet. Still, the child should have room to move around a bit.
3. Mattress Must be sturdy – and fit snug inside the crib to prevent open spaces on the sides in which little limbs can become stuck. Remove all pillows and other loose objects.

4. Room Make sure it's well-ventilated even in winter, and not too warm (about 65 degrees Fahrenheit, 18 degrees Celsius).
5. Stuffed toy Let your baby get acquainted with a stuffed animal, perhaps during mealtimes. Buy an extra copy to prevent dramas in case the original goes AWOL. Bonding between the child and his favorite cuddly toy can occur after 9 to 12 months.
6. Night light
7. Music box Simple, high-pitched melodies have a soothing effect on babies.

Optimum charge

Obtain your product's optimum charge with the following activities:

1. Expose him to the outside air
Environmental temperature changes will increase the baby's appetite, resistance to diseases, and induce good sleep behavior. Your baby will thrive if you take him outside two to three hours a day, preferably in the middle of the day between meals.

2. Play More stimulation equals more sleep. But don't overdo it – your child can get overtired and find it more difficult to drift off. Don't rack your brains trying to come up with just the right game. To a baby, just watching and discovering a face is a fascinating way to spend hours.

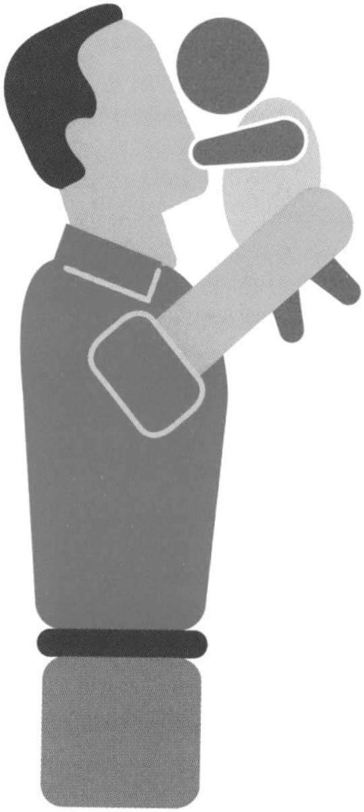

3. Regular schedule Establish a steady routine around feeding and bathing your baby. This goes double for sleep time rituals. The same sequence of events every evening provides a soothing kind of stability that will calm your child and help him fall asleep.

4. Father puts baby down It can be helpful for the dad to put the baby to bed. It gives your producer a break and the baby may settle more easily away from the smell of the mother's milk.

Charging rhythm

Your product recharges during short and long intervals of rest and sleep.

Sleep frequency Your child doesn't yet have the ability to distinguish day from night. Most babies sleep in relatively brief spurts – 10-minute naps, 2-hour siestas, nighttime sleep periods of 3 to 4 hours. Because the child's stomach is still on the small side, he'll want to be fed with great frequency. The intervals between meals get longer as stomach capacity increases. At 3 months, he may sleep for up to 6 hours at a time. After 6 to 13 weeks, the need for nighttime feedings lessens and some, but not all, babies sleep through the night.

Sleep quantity In the first month, babies sleep most of the time – 12 to 15 hours a day. After a month, that reduces by about an hour. After half a year, the baby sleeps 14 hours; after one year, 13. The amount of sleep needed stays more or less constant in the child's early life; most five-year-olds still sleep about 12 hours a day.

Day versus night A newborn sleeps as well during the day as during the night. Gradually acclimatize your child to the difference between day and night by leaving the curtains or blinds open during the daytime.

Waking up A baby sleeps for as long as he needs to; there's no need to wake him up. Sometimes, babies wake up unexpectedly in the middle of the night. This often happens during periods of teething and growing pains, or when they've just begun to master a new skill (crawling or standing). Just like adults, babies have phases of deep and light sleep throughout the night, but they cycle more rapidly in infants. About 20 minutes after falling asleep, the baby goes into a deeper sleep that lasts an hour to 90 minutes, after which a less-deep phase occurs – REM (rapid eye movement) sleep. The eyelids may undulate with the movement of the eyes behind them, which seemingly scan from side to side almost as if following an object. During this period, increased brain activity occurs (the blood pumped to the brain doubles in volume), often leading to dreaming. The fact that babies, too, experience this REM phase, leads some researchers to believe that babies do in fact dream. The transition from deep sleep to REM sleep marks the moment when it's most likely for your baby to wake up. If he wakes and makes a sound, wait for a moment before picking him up – some babies fall back asleep on their own. If he wakes more fully and calls for you, go ahead and comfort him. In adults, one sleep cycle (from light to deep sleep and back again) takes roughly 90 minutes. A baby will go through the same cycle in 50 to 60 minutes. Each hour, he crosses that sensitive threshold between deep and light sleep.

Loading dock

Your product needs a safe, sheltered location to get the necessary rest. The American Academy of Pediatrics recommends that babies sleep in their parents' room for the first 6 months. Choose from the following options:

Bassinet

A safe bassinet has these specs:

- Roughly 12 inches deep, 18 inches wide, 32 inches long
- No sharp edges
- For standing models: make sure the stand is sturdy and won't tip
- Side walls, or bars spaced two to two-and-a-half inches apart

Every bassinet is required to meet official safety requirements. Make sure yours does. You will also need a waterproof mattress cover and at least three fitted sheets. You'll need the bassinet for only about three months, depending on how fast your baby grows. As soon as the baby can sit, kneel, or pull himself up, it's advisable to change the loading options.

Crib

You may skip the bassinet altogether and put the baby to sleep in a crib instead. These guidelines apply:

- Measures roughly 47 to 55 inches in length, 24 wide
- Mattress support consists of planks or a perforated wooden board
- Side walls 22 inches or more, distance between bars two to two and a half inches
- Smooth surfaces all over – no splinters, knobs, screws, or other protuberances

Your bed

Many experts believe that there is no more natural location for a baby to sleep than the parents' bed. It's hard to argue with that theory. In traditional cultures, mother and baby sleep together, and that's how our stone-age ancestors did it. There's even some evidence suggesting that the rise of postpartum depression is the result of having babies sleep separately from their mothers. Apart from the natural closeness and bonding that occurs when the baby sleeps in your bed, there's the advantage that neither parent will have to get up in the middle of the night to comfort or feed the child. A hungry baby sleeping close to mom will find his way to the breast. If you intend to share your bed with your child, here are some tips:

- A hard mattress is preferable to a soft one (or a waterbed).
- Remove pillows and heavy comforters and give the baby a light blanket.
- Put the baby between the two of you. You and your producer form the natural boundaries of the bed.
- Don't leave your child in the parental bed all by himself.

Separate room

Unless you have a good reason to want to continue with the baby sharing your bed, it's a good idea to give the child his own room after about 9 months. Wait longer than that, and your baby will become enough of a creature of habit to fiercely resist adapting to another sleep arrangement. You can also put the baby in his room from the get-go, provided that you'll be close by to listen for problems.

Sleep tips for Baby Managers

If your baby really doesn't want to go to sleep, he might have a sleep disorder. A rare if worrisome phenomenon is sleep apnea – an affliction that interrupts breathing during sleep. The word apnea comes from the Latin and refers to not breathing. A child with apnea will probably wake up a lot because of his lack of regular breathing. The cause of the apnea is the abnormal relaxation of the muscles of the airway during deep sleep. Sleep apnea can be damaging to the brain. See your pediatrician if your child sleeps poorly and frequently snores and breathes loudly in his sleep.

Bedtime music

Several semi-scientific studies reveal that babies drift off to sleep better when they hear a monotone sound at a level just below that of a vacuum cleaner. There's a simple reason for it: the baby associates the sound with that of the womb, where it spent nine months listening to the rushing of the mother's blood accompanied by a bass rhythm of the heart beating in the background. Many music producers have captured this sound with the aid of tiny microphones. Some have "translated" the beat of the womb into instrumental sounds, while others have released recordings in which the ambient track serves as a backdrop onto which other sounds have been layered. Whether such music will have a positive effect on your baby falling asleep depends on the infant. Most babies can appreciate simple, soothing, rhythmic sounds – but then again, it's not unheard of for a baby to nod off blissfully to wailing guitar solos, heavy dance music, or – wonder of wonders – total silence. Babies are already individuals, after all, with their own idiosyncrasies and preferences. Nonetheless, it's a reasonable assumption that sounds from the womb have a calming effect on very young children.

More info:

www.bastamusic.com: The Dutch specialty label has re-released the classic recordings from the baby-music genre. The American pianist, band leader, and composer Raymond Scott (1908-1994), an electronic-music pioneer when Brian Eno and Kraftwerk were still in diapers, created all kinds of melodies meant to put babies to sleep. The music was played on instruments that Scott developed himself – contraptions with names like Clavivox and the Electronium. The *Soothing Sounds for Babies* collection consists of three CDs: one for newborns, one for babies older than six months, and one for 12-to-18-month-olds. With the true purist and audiophile in mind, Basta has also pressed Soothing Sounds on vinyl, in the original album sleeves and accompanied by the booklet that was part of the early-sixties release. More information about Raymond Scott can be found at **www.raymondscott.com**.

www.musicforbabies.net: Site of Advanced Brain technologies from Ogden, Utah. The institute has released a series of CDs of primarily classical music that purports to stimulate babies' brain development.

www.music4babies.com: Site of Veldhoven (the Netherlands) composer Raimond Lap; he creates music, fairy tales, and videos for babies and young children.

www.purewhitenoise.com: Big online store that offers a choice of all kinds of white noise – a kind of soundless sound. Here you can buy CDs featuring the sounds of hairdryers and vacuum cleaners.

Mobile mode

Your baby literally can't get anywhere without your help. Here's how to activate his mobile mode.

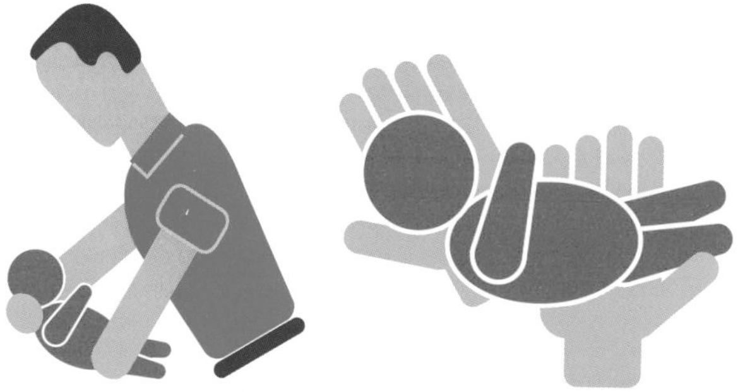

Vertically

Put one hand under neck and head (neck muscles are barely developed at first, so make sure the head doesn't loll). Place your other hand so that it supports his back and buttocks. Lift the baby to your chest.

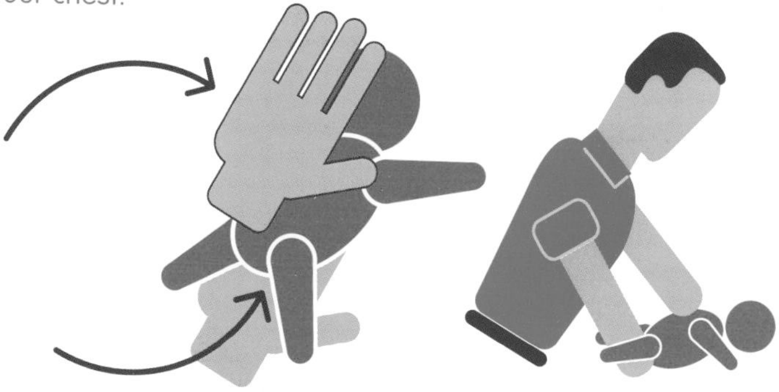

Horizontally

Turn your baby onto his belly. Place your hand on his chest after reaching your arm between his legs. Your other hand goes firmly on the baby's back. Lift.

Rocking

Always hold the baby in your left arm: he'll be soothed by your heartbeat. Place your right hand under his head and neck and your left under his buttocks and back. Move your right hand toward your left arm, cradle the baby's head in the crook of your elbow, and let his body rest on your underarm.

Throwing

It's a common thing for new parents, an expression of exuberance: playfully toss and catch the baby, launching him straight up into the air. One word: don't. There have been cases of au pairs being convicted for manslaughter after they shook the babies in their care. Since then, several studies have been done to determine the effects of tumbling and shaking on a baby's brain. The verdict: even innocent-looking behavior such as playfully throwing the baby up in the air can lead to accidental brain damage. The phenomenon is known as Shaken Baby Syndrome, something that occurs after the brain hits the inside of the skull, possibly triggering nerve damage in the neck. The consequences can be very serious, including paralysis, speech abnormalities, and cognitive problems.

Mobile accessories – baby carrying

A sharp-tongued columnist once likened the baby carrier to a modern father's penis gourd. The sneer was aimed at a journalist who wrote about the female attention he received when he stepped out with his infant cradled in such a device. Although baby carriers may seem modern, they go back to ancient times and in many cultures this method of transportation is still the norm. From China to India to Indonesia, babies are carried this way. 'Babywearing' can be a great way for dads to bond with their offspring, support their partners and learn how to respond to their child's need for comfort. If a baby suffers from colic or reflux, time spent being carried by their father can be a lifesaver for everyone.

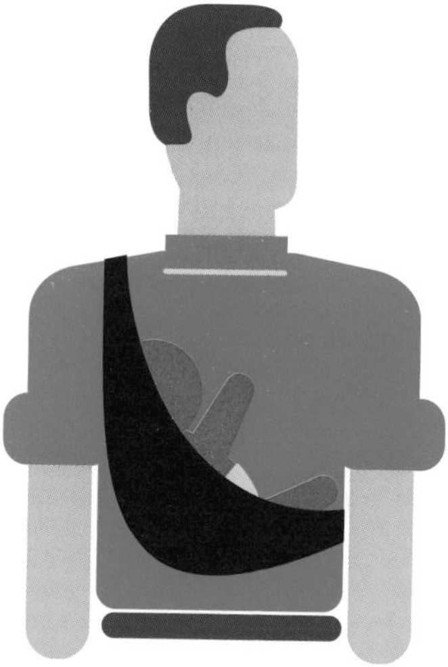

Sling

Using a sling means you can cuddle your baby while your hands are free to do other things. There are lots of soft slings suitable for use from birth, such as pouches, ring slings and stretchy or woven wraps. They all work on the same principle: position your baby in the fold of cloth, pull it in snugly and ensure your baby has their head and neck supported with their chin off their chest.

Front carrier

When your baby is a few months old you might like to try a buckle carrier (although some are suitable from birth). The baby is carried on your front, facing in, and the straps go over your shoulders and around your waist. Look for one where the baby is seated with his legs in a 'froggy' position rather than dangling straight down.

Back carrier

Many buckle carriers can also be used on your back, or you can buy hiking backpack carriers. It's best to wait until your baby has good head and neck control before back-carrying.

Less crying

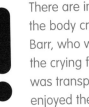

There are indications that babies who are often carried against the body cry less. The Canadian child psychiatrist Ronald Barr, who works at Montreal's McGill University, compared the crying frequency of two groups of babies: one group that was transported in a body carrier 2 hours a day, and one that enjoyed the same treatment for 4 hours a day. Infants in the latter group cried 43 per cent less.

Mobile mode: packaging

Protection from heat and sun

The outside of your product is very sensitive to sunlight. During the first six months you shouldn't use sun protection lotions, as your baby's skin might not tolerate them yet. After six months, use oil or lotion with an SPF of at least 15. When the sun is shining and you take your child out for a stroll, dress him in light-colored, loose-fitting clothes that cover the whole body. Don't forget to put socks on him, and cover his head in a hat with a wide, floppy brim. Use an umbrella over the stroller.

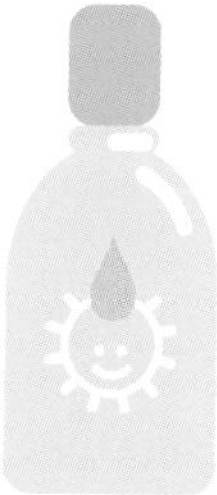

Protection from ice and cold

Unless the newscast talking heads show images of five-foot icicles and take obvious relish in using the term *wind chill factor*, your baby doesn't need to be cooped up during the winter months. Package him in a warm hat, gloves, and booties, as well as a winter coat and, if needed, a blanket.

Material and provisions

Whenever you take the baby out of the house, have the following ready:

- food (if needed)
- Bottle of sterilized drinking water
- Toys
- Diapers and wipes
- A change of clothes
- Stuffed animal

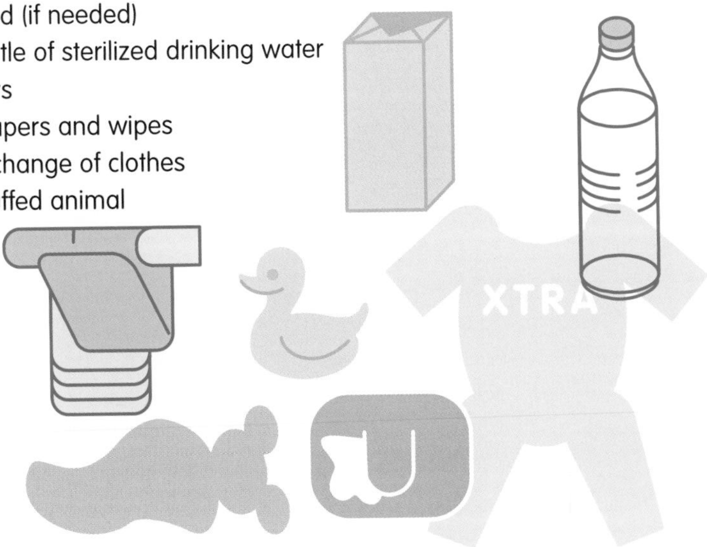

Mobile tips for Baby Managers

- Because they have subcutaneous insulating fat, and because their sweat glands do not function yet, babies are quick to overheat. You have to see to it that your child neither cools down nor heats up to much. The color of the face gives much away. A baby who's hot becomes red and splotchy; one who's cold is on the pale side.
- You can sense the temperature by placing two fingers behind the baby's neck. If everything seems normal, it probably is.
- Sun rays are actually healthy for your child (because they help the generation of vitamin D in the skin). Just don't overdo it. Let your child acclimatize to the sun over time. Start with just five minutes.
- If you plan to go outside when it's cold, place a hot-water bottle in the stroller a few minutes before you leave.

Transportation mode

All sorts of wheeled transportation devices have been developed to enable you to move your product from A to B. Base your choice on criteria such as weight, size, cost, functionality, and durability. Always test-drive your intended purchase before plonking down your hard-earned cash. If you decide on a collapsible model, check if it fits in your car trunk.

The old timer

When to use: Immediately.

Model: With its large spoke wheels and oversized undercarriage, this is a Cadillac for babies. It's still a subject of debate who invented the original "perambulator" or "pram." Was it the English architect William Kent who designed the vehicle for the children of the third Duke of Devonshire, in 1733? Or might it have been Charles Burton who, in 1848, amazed and annoyed New York pedestrians with his rolling contraptions? Perhaps the pram is really the brainchild of a German entrepreneur, Ernst Albert Naether, who managed to build a veritable pram industry in the middle of the 19th century. Whatever the truth, the choice of an old timer is a choice for elegance and tradition.

Pros:

- Retro look with a high attention quotient
- Pampered transportation with good protection from the elements
- Solid "investment"

Cons:

- Big, usually doesn't fold, vulnerable
- No factory warranty if it's a real "antique"
- No modern gizmos

Price: There's a lively second-hand market for these collectibles. Restored ones start at about $150. Some of the most seductive beauties in this category can be found in the collection of the world's only Victorian Perambulator Museum in Jefferson, Ohio.

Stroller

When to use: Now.

Model: With this successor to the classic perambulator, you can start promenading soon after the baby's birth. Because their spines are not yet well-developed, young babies are not supposed to be transported in sitting or reclining positions for more than 90 minutes at a time. Like the prams of old, strollers are ideal because they enable the child to be transported in a prone position. That's all that the traditional models do, while modern varieties may have features that "grow" as the baby gets older, like the ability to be converted to a sitting position. Some models boast a detachable travel crib; when the child outgrows the crib, the undercarriage can be used for a stroller seat insert.

Pros:

- Comfortable and offers plenty of protection for the very young
- Supremely practical
- The convertible models can be used until the child is 3 or 4 years old.

Cons:

- Pricey, especially the combination models

Price: From $200 to $1,000.

Jogging stroller

When to use: from 6 to 12 months.

Model: Despite the modern-sounding name, a 3-wheeled baby carriage is an old idea. Because vehicles were once taxed according to the number of wheels, designers went for 3-wheel designs with 2 rear wheels and 1 in front. Current models are being targeted at a relatively upscale, sporty audience. Children can sit or lie down in one of these.

Pros:

- Looks sporty
- Collapsible

Cons:

- May require considerable pushing power

Price: Roughly ranges from $100 to $600.

Umbrella stroller

When to use: from 7 to 12 months.

Model: The umbrella stroller was developed in the 60s and is now in its 5th decade. Its longevity has a lot to do with its convenience: they are light, compact, and easy to transport when not in use. Then again, they constrain kids in fairly narrow seats and don't provide much in the way of springs or shocks.

Pros:

- Terrifically practical. With the right hardware they can even be transported on bikes
- Folds flat
- Adjustable back

Cons:

- Child can't lie flat
- Lacks creature comforts

Price: From $15 to $300.

Buying tips

In general

- Take a look at your neighborhood and picture yourself navigating the roads and sidewalks with your chosen baby vehicle. Are the ground surfaces smooth or rough? How tall are the sidewalks? Are there ramps for strollers and wheelchairs?
- Spring for a sturdier stroller if you'll be going on nature walks. Chances are you won't take junior mountain-climbing just yet, but air-filled tires and largish wheels do come in handy on uneven and muddy forest paths.
- The brake should work on at least 2 wheels. Make sure it is situated out of the baby's reach, preferably on the handles or the push bar. When the brake is engaged, the stroller should stay put when you lean or push against it.
- Small caster-type wheels are handy and practical in cities. Look for ones that are outfitted with shocks, and make sure you can lock the wheels in position.
- Choose non-spoke wheels, or wheels with covers, to eliminate the chance of little fingers getting stuck and bloodied.
- Pay attention to how tightly the stroller turns – the smaller the diameter of the circle, the better.
- Stability matters more than the ultimate in maneuverability. Make sure the stroller doesn't easily flip when another kid pulls on it, or when your child leans over the edge.
- Is the push bar height-adjustable? That's an advantage if you're

tall. And is it reversible? That's a boon if you want to pull the stroller – in soft sand or slushy snow for instance.

- Can the seat or basket be positioned either way – forward- or rearward-facing? It's nice to have the option.
- Can the seat back be locked in at last three positions?
- To keep your child from breathing in lots of exhaust fumes, it helps if the seat or basket is at least 16 to 20 inches off the ground.
- Convertible models are convenient in ways you might have to see to truly understand the benefits. Have a sales person demonstrate these advantages to you, and try out the mechanism yourself. Pay special attention to the safety and easy operation of the locking feature that prevents the stroller from folding/collapsing.
- Try opening and closing the stroller. Does it need to be lifted in the process? If so, that could put a strain on your back.
- Is the upholstery removable and washable?
- For safety belts to work properly, they should be at least .75 inches wide.
- Make sure there are no rivets, tacks, or metal decorations that could hurt you or your child.
- Before you buy, take a close look at the instructions. They should be clear and complete and not induce "Ikea rage".

Accessories

- The rain shield that comes with your stroller should have sufficient ventilation.
- A mosquito net, an umbrella, and a bag-type leg wrap are handy to have. The umbrella can also be angled to protect against the wind, and the mosquito net keeps insects, such as bees and wasps, at bay too.
- Finally, a separate carry bag can be a practical accessory. Some can be clipped to the stroller's frame.

1. Head support
2. Wings
3. Position in the center of the back seat
4. Instruction and safety information label
5. 5-point belt

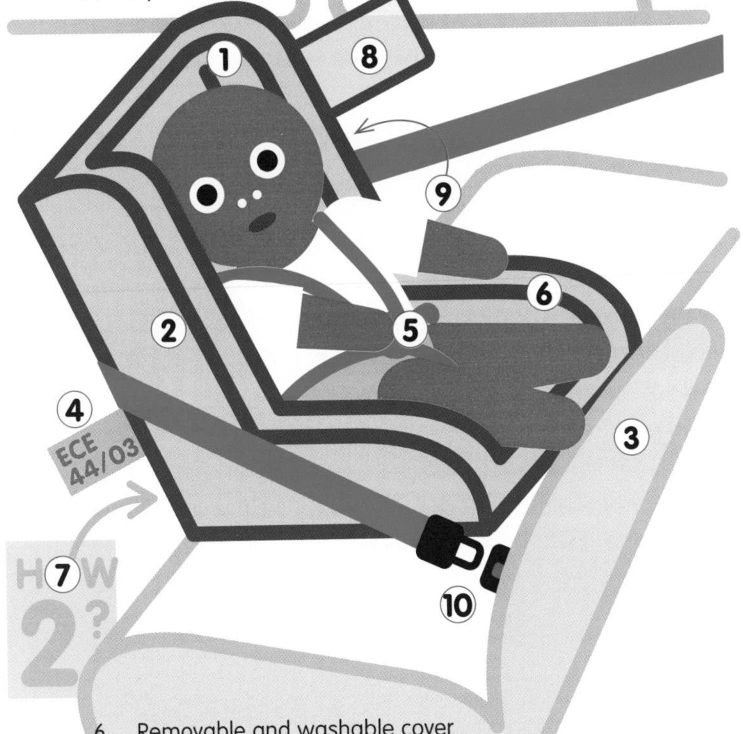

6. Removable and washable cover
7. Manual
8. Sun visor
9. Arched back, limit length of travel time
10. Sturdy buckles or anchors for stability

Mobile mode with motorized transport

For car-based transportation, you'll need a kind of Goldilocks chair for your product: not too small, not too large, but just right. Make your selection based on safety and ease of installation.

Most western countries now require child safety seats, whether your child sits in the front or the back. In general, if your child is shorter than 4.5 feet (53 inches), he'll need a child seat or a booster seat. Kids who are taller just need the standard three-point seatbelt.

In Europe, a new ruling was enforced in January 2006. Under this regulation you are obliged to transport children smaller than 1.35 meters in a safety child-seat or booster-seat. Children bigger than 1.35 meters must – just like adults – use a seat belt. So it is compulsory for children smaller than 1.35 to ride in a safety child-seat or booster-seat. If the kids sit up front or in back is not the issue any more, but the use of a safety child-seat is obligatory. Brussels also makes demands on the safety child-seat. The seat must comply with regulation ECE 40/03. In the U.S. child safety-seat requirements vary according to state law. Check the regulations for your state.

Recently a new universal system has been developed: Isofix. With one click the safety child-seat is anchored to the back seat. Many modern cars now support this design. Consult your car's user-manual before purchasing this option.

Weight sizing

Determining which safety child-seat your child needs, depends on his weight. There are five sizes:

Size	Weight	Age
0	< 22 lb	to 9 months
0+	< 29 lb	to 18 months
1	20-40 lb	9 months to 3 years
2	2-55 lb	3–6 years
3	49-80 lb	6–10 years

Airbags and how to position your child

It's not advisable – and in some countries it's against the law – to transport a child in the front, facing forward, even when he's strapped into a child seat. That's because if the airbags deploy, the force of the blast could be fatal to your young passenger. Even if your car gives you the option to disable the passenger-side front airbag with the push of a button, don't chance it: in rare cases, a switched-off airbag can still deploy.

Another safety consideration should be how the child seat is positioned – forward- or rearward-facing. Child seats facing the rear tend to be the safest in frontal crashes, when the seat's head support absorbs a good deal of the blow, also preventing serious whiplash and other neck injuries. As a rule, all children up to 12 months should be transported in rearward-facing car seats.

Buying tips

- Don't buy a second-hand child safety seat, due to possible hidden defects.
- Take your child to the store. Before you commit to buying him

a particular seat, place the seat in your car and assess the ease of installation and the quality of the hardware. The seat must be so stable as to be practically impossible to move. Now place your child in the seat and make sure he can be comfortably secured. Are the belts adjustable to suit his height? Is the hip belt sufficiently low on his frame? Make sure the seat is equipped with a five-point belt, so that your child can't "submarine" (slide out from under the shoulder and hip straps).

- Does the seat have a reclining position so that your child can nap comfortably?
- Is the upholstery removable and washable? If the cover does get permanently soiled or damaged, can you replace it, rather than buy a whole new seat?
- Carefully peruse the instructions. While you're at it, also consult your car's manual and see what it says about child safety.

User tips

- Position the child seat in the middle of the car's back seat: that's the safest spot in case of a side-impact collision.
- Follow the seat manufacturer's instructions to the letter. Many child traffic fatalities are the result of incorrect child-seat installations.
- Remove the road atlas, the bobblehead figurine, and other loose objects from the shelf under the rear window.
- If you have a small infant, roll up two towels and place them on either side of your baby next to the armrests.
- Make sure the belts are tight while still keeping your child comfortable.
- Get your baby used to the car. Wait a few weeks before you

take him on car trips and start with short rides. Gradually increase the duration.

- Make sure baby is sitting or lying with a well supported (arched) lower back, as this is the most secure position in case of accident. Limit trips in the car to about 1–2 hours during the first year. When unavoidable, divide up longer trips with regular breaks.
- Don't adjust the child seat while you're driving.
- Baby stores sell special mirrors that let you keep an eye on your child in the back seat without requiring you to turn around.
- Don't park in the scorching sun if you can help it, as the child seat (and your own) can get painfully hot.
- Frequently adjust the child seat to accommodate your offspring's size and weight increase.
- Always use the child seat, no exceptions. When your offspring realizes this is not negotiable, the seat will cease to be an issue. Most child traffic fatalities occur because parents underestimate the risks of not consistently following the safety guidelines.
- Children aged four to 12 are exposed to the biggest risk, as they are often too big for child seats and not yet big enough for a standard three-point belt.

Input

4 Input

Super cocktail

Try to make sure that your product gets breast milk for at least the first six months. Research shows pretty irrefutably that breastfeeding yields a net profit, health-wise – both short-term and long-term. The following aids might come in handy when administering the super cocktail:

1. Feeding pillow Boomerang-shaped pillow that hugs the mother's torso and supports the baby during his meal.

2. Feeding bra Functional brassiere, often of cotton and lace, that facilitates access to the breasts via foldaway flaps with buttons, snaps, or zippers. Makes it unnecessary for the mother to take off the whole bra, and helps dry her nipples after feeding. Available in various sizes and models, though not, it seems, in leather or latex.

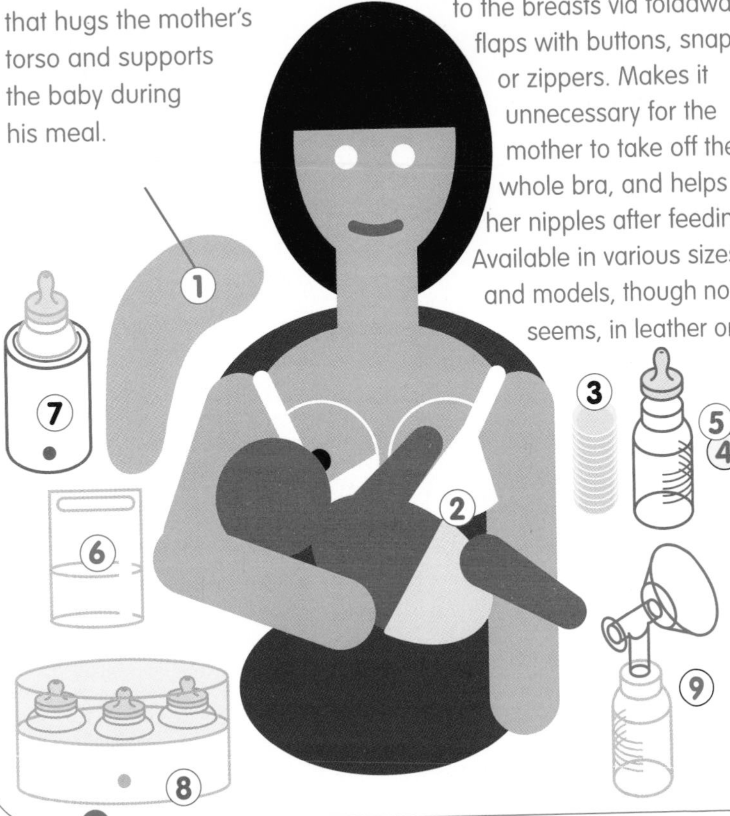

3. Breast pads If the breasts leak somewhat, these absorbent pads wick away the moisture. Available as washables and disposables.
4. Bottle Silicone or glass bottle for keeping or serving mother's milk. Also suitable for administering baby formula. Breast milk has a limited shelf life: you can keep it in the fridge for up to 72 hours (below 39°F) or in the freezer for about six months (at zero degrees or lower).
5. Nipple Made of rubber or silicone, this mouthpiece can be screwed onto the bottle; it controls the flow of the milk with a number of small holes. Some models come with an air canal that prevents the nipple from collapsing under the baby's suction, by allowing air to flow between the inside and outside of the bottle.
6. Bag for expressed milk When expressing (pumping) breast milk for freezing, this bag holds the liquid. After thawing, can be easily placed in a bottle for administering.
7. Bottle warmer Thaws bags of frozen milk, bottles, and jars, and warms them to the desired temperature. Some models feature a car adapter, which might come in handy if the baby gets hungry in a traffic jam.
8. Sterilizer Bottles, pacifiers, and nipples ought to be sterilized often. First rinse them under hot tap water, then boil them in a pan for a little while. Too much trouble? There are alternatives, such as a steam sterilizer that gets rid of germs and other microscopic evildoers in 9 minutes, treating 6 bottles at a time; or a microwave sterilizer which, true to its name, works in a standard household microwave oven.
9. Breast pump Mechanical or electrical contraption that helps remove breast milk by pumping the liquid into a funnel, an activity that's sometimes called "expressing" milk. The milk lands in a bottle or a storage bag and is frozen for future use. Some models double up on the pumping action, tapping two breasts at once.

Breastfeeding

The production of the super cocktail is a delicate, elaborate process involving muscles, hormones, and brains – those of both the mother and the baby.

The basic building blocks of breast milk are primarily delivered through the bloodstream. During the 9-month assembly of your product, hormones called estrogen, progesterone, and prolactin (1) stimulate

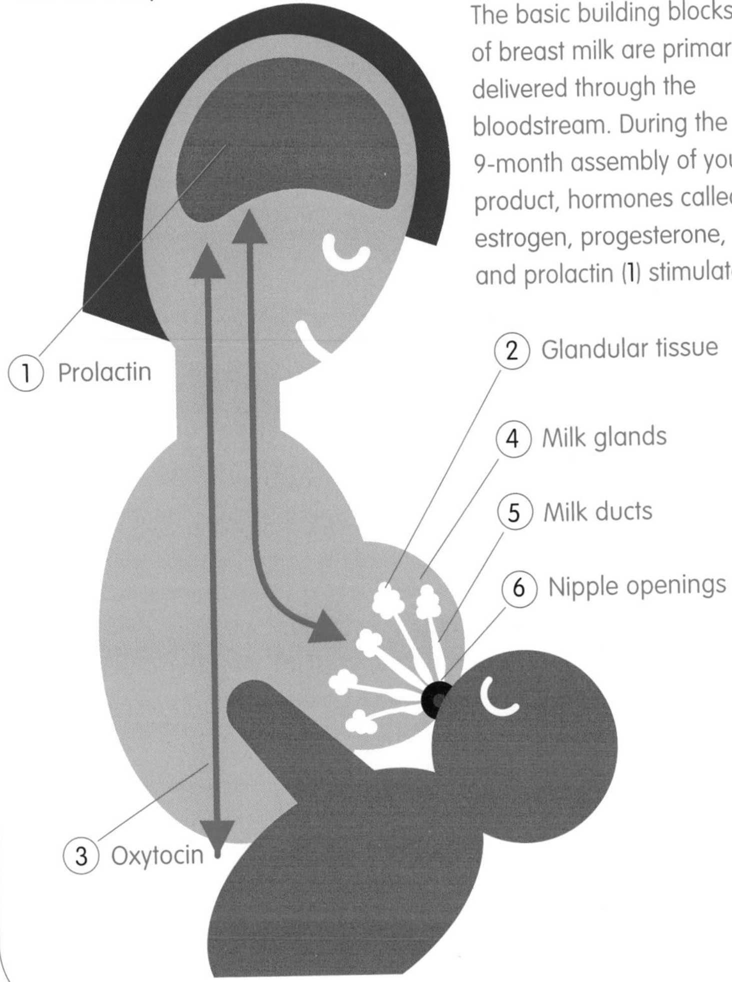

the growth of glandular tissue (2) in the breast. Immediately after the delivery of the baby, the relative hormone levels change drastically: estrogen and progesterone levels go down, prolactin levels go up. This now-dominant hormone brings about the so-called secretion phase, with actual milk production close behind. Triggered by the baby's suckling, another hormone enters the mix: the pituitary gland starts producing oxytocin (3), leading to the contraction of muscles around the milk glands (4). These muscles propel the milk outward, through tiny ducts (5) that lead to the nipple openings (6) where it becomes available to the baby.

Kinds of milk

As soon as the baby starts to drink, he gets the "foremilk": a low-fat watery substance loaded with vitamins and minerals – the perfect thirst-quencher. As the feed progresses, the fat content of the milk increases. In the first days after delivery, breast milk is sometimes known as colostrum. It has a uniquely yellowish tint and is rich in immune factors. It also has a laxative effect. In other words, colostrum facilitates the baby's first output.

Breastfeeding numbers

During feeding and in between feedings, prolactin stimulates the production of new milk. The more the baby drinks, the more milk is produced. Immediately after the delivery (preferably within an hour), skin-to-skin contact between mother and child is of vital importance, in part because it stimulates milk production.

The chemical make-up of the milk – the ratio of ingredients – **does** change, however; the producer adapts what she produces to the baby's exact needs.

Breastfeeding and diet

Breast milk is made indirectly from what the mother ingests. You can help her pay attention to the following tips.

The relationship between the quality of your partner's meals and the breast milk she produces is not as clear-cut as many people assume. Evolution protects the child from a mother who, for whatever reason, doesn't eat properly. Breast milk's consistency and ingredients are, for a long time, virtually independent of the mother's own food. Only if she is seriously malnourished will the quality of the milk suffer. On the other hand, the milk's taste and aroma may be influenced by your producer's diet.

Toxic substances

The guideline above is true in a broad-stroke kind of way, which isn't to say that there are no substances that, when used heavily, could influence the quality of breast milk. Even small quantities of alcohol show up in mother's milk. Research has shown that babies don't like alcohol and that they'll drink less breast milk if it contains alcohol. Still, it's hard to see how the occasional alcoholic beverage would have a detrimental effect on mother or baby. The human body breaks down a serving of alcohol in about 1.5 to 2 hours. After that time, it's gone from breast milk too. If your partner would like a glass of wine, no problem, but encourage her to feed the baby (or pump milk) first. Caffeinated products such as coffee and cola can make the baby unsettled and fussy. Taken in moderation, caffeine is unlikely to be a big problem, however. A couple of cups/ glasses a day is fine. About the effects of other substances, including onions, various spices, different kinds of cabbage, orange juice, and chocolate, not much is known. Simply put, babies differ. If you notice a connection between a certain food and any intestinal problems your baby develops, ask your partner to modify her diet. In general, spices are not known to cause trouble.

Positive influences

"Swallow worms with honey wine, feast on the breasts of animals that produce much milk, or mix a bat's or owl's ashes with water and rub it into the breasts." That's a thousand-year-old Gallic recipe for wet nurses. Silly rumors and quackery persist regarding substances intended to stimulate the production of breast milk – such as the positive effects attributed to drinking aniseed tea or dark beer. Neither actually help with breast milk production.

Extra energy

A breastfeeding woman needs extra energy and nutrients. A varied diet with some additional helpings of bread and fruit usually suffices, although a vitamin D deficiency is still a possibility. If your partner only breastfeeds for a few weeks, no extra vitamin D is necessary; longer than that, and she'd do well to take at least 400 iu a day, perhaps in the form of a multivitamin pill. It's also important that she drinks enough to avoid feeling thirsty.

Facts and myths about breastfeeding

Myth: It'll make my partner's breasts sag.
Fact: Changes in the shape and size of the breasts are caused by hormonal changes the body goes through during the assembly process. Whether or not your partner breastfeeds has no bearing on the shape or firmness of the breasts after delivery.

Myth: As long as my partner breastfeeds, she won't feel like having sex.
Fact: The moment your partner becomes interested in sex again is determined mostly by the course of the pregnancy, how fast she recovers, and how much her circumstances change. Breastfeeding can sometimes actually awaken the senses; the hormone oxytocin, which is released during feeding, plays an important part in lovemaking too.

Myth: Formula is just as good and nutritious as breast milk.
Fact: Formula lacks important ingredients that help a baby build up resistance to illness. But formula is a fine alternative if your partner is unable to produce (sufficient) milk.

Myth: A breastfed child does not eat as much as it needs.
Fact: Milk production works according to the principle of supply and demand. The body makes extra milk for babies who are especially hungry.

Myth: Breastfeeding cannot be combined with having a job.
Fact: Admittedly, it's a challenge. In most countries, though not the U.S. (so far), employers are obliged by law to provide a suitable private space and (paid) time for a mother who wishes to breastfeed her child or pump milk. In the Netherlands, women are permitted to spend up to a quarter of their total working hours on these activities. The World Health Organization and UNICEF both strongly encourage employers to facilitate the continuation of breastfeeding when women return to work.

Methods and frequency

The holy grail of breastfeeding is getting a "good latch" or connection between the mother's breast and the baby's mouth; this will prevent frustrations for both parties.

Positioning This may take some trial and error. The baby is outfitted with a reflex that makes him latch onto the breast and suckle. If it doesn't seem to happen as naturally as all that, try these tips:

- Make sure that mother and child are comfortable and well-supported.
- Hold the baby's head slightly upright to give it the opportunity to explore the area with its face and find the nipple.
- The touch of the nipple stimulates the opening of the child's lips. When that occurs, the child can be brought in closer to the breast.
- After a few short suckling motions, the child begins to drink bigger mouthfuls. If all is well, there'll be a soothing rhythm to the baby's suckling and swallowing.
- If breastfeeding is painful, or your partner is worried that she is not producing enough milk, seek support from an International Board Certified Lactation Consultant (IBCLC), or peer counselor from La Leche League, Breastfeeding USA, or WIC. To find an IBCLC near you, go to **www.ilca.org**.

! Your partner may need time, as well as peace and quiet, in order to get the hang of breastfeeding. Guide proud grandparents and other potential onlookers to another room.

On demand or on schedule? In the first half of the previous century, women were warned not to feed their babies too often. The prevailing medical opinion was that mothers ought to conform to a strict feeding schedule. Nowadays, feeding-on-cue is the norm. Flexibility is fine. During the first few weeks, the baby will nurse 8 to 12 times per 24-hour day. If the child steadily gains weight and produces plenty of wet and poopy diapers, mother and child are on the right track. After roughly 3 months, nighttime feeding becomes a thing of the past for some babies: finally everyone can get a decent night's sleep again!

Baby formula

Despite investments of many millions, the food industry has still not managed to copy mother's milk. Formula does improve a little each year as new research is implemented. It's a fact that children raised on formula grow normally; it's not entirely clear, however, whether they develop their physical, emotional and intellectual capacity optimally. Breast milk is a dynamic food that changes as the individual child's needs change. Formula will probably always be a "static," unchanging source of food, and its long-term effects on children are as yet poorly understood. In the table below you'll find the most important differences.

Nutrients	Mother's milk	Formula
Fats are crucial nutrients in mother's milk, stimulating development of the brain and the nervous system. They contain essential fatty acids and an enzyme, lipase, that breaks down the fat into smaller globules so it can be better absorbed into the bloodstream.	Contains fatty acids DHA (docosahexaenoic acid) and AA (arachidonic acid), important building blocks for brain development and vision. Quantities vary during a feeding. Rich in cholesterol (20 mg/dl).	Does not always contain DHA. Fat level is unchanging. Contains no cholesterol.
Proteins are large molecules consisting of amino acids that are strung together like beads on a necklace. Amino acids are essential for the production of body-specific proteins.	Contains lactoferrin, a protein with antimicrobial properties that regulates iron intake. Contains lysozyme, a bacteria-fighting protein.	Contains almost no lactoferrin, and no lysozyme.
Proteins also play a big part in a good number of physiological processes, such as forming a shield against infections and helping keep the colon healthy.	Contains immunoglobulins such as sIgA, which offers protection against infections of the airways and the colon.	Contains no immunoglobulins

Carbohydrates provide energy. Oligosaccharides are natural substances that help the colon function and keep infections at bay.	Contains many kinds of oligosaccharides.	Certain brands contain a few oligosaccharides.
Vitamins and minerals	The level of minerals is low, but their absorption is high. Low on vitamins K and D.	The absorption of minerals is lower, but the levels are higher. Sufficient vitamins K and D.
Hormones stimulate the biochemical balance.	Rich in a range of hormones such as thyroid, prolactin, oxytocin and more than fifteen others.	Contains no hormones.
Taste	Varies depending on the mother's diet, so that the baby develops different taste patterns. This is an advantage when introducing new foods to the child.	Always the same. The baby doesn't learn that food can taste different from meal to meal.
Cost	About $650 a year (in extra food for the mother).	From $1,300 for standard formula to $2,600 for special products such as hypoallergenic formula. Plus costs for bottles and supplies.

Extra vitamins

Breast milk is low in vitamins K and D. A vitamin K deficiency can lead to problems with blood coagulation. That's why many newborns receive extra vitamin K. It's generally a good idea to administer three daily drops of a vitamin K solution during the baby's first three months. Extra vitamin D is also advisable, starting in the third week of the baby's life. Ask your pediatrician for his or her recommendation, including advice on dosage.

Choosing formula

Formula is available in all kinds of versions and brands. To enable you to make a choice among them without first getting a degree in biochemistry, here is what you need to know.

Fats The fat in formula consists of vegetable oils. The consistency of these, and their proportion to each other, may be slightly different between brands, but all brands have fat levels that are comparable to those in breast milk. The oils are not a source of cholesterol. Sometimes, manufacturers add AA and DHA to the formula. Research into the mental acuity of 8-year-olds revealed that children who'd been breastfed had a higher IQ than children raised on formula without AA and DHA. This remained true even after the researchers eliminated noise factors such as the educational and income level of the parents. The cause for this difference seems to have everything to do with DHA. Not so long ago, scientists believed that babies were able to make their own DHA from various fatty acids, but large-scale tests have indicated reliably that breastfed children have the edge when it comes to DHA levels. There have been elaborate discussions between food manufacturers and health authorities about the most effective and safest way to add DHA to formula. Some firms have developed a patented technology resulting in DHA that closely resembles the naturally-occurring DHA in breast milk.

More info: www.askdrsears.com – the site of pediatrician William Sears, who has delved into this matter like no other expert.

Proteins The most important differences are in the proportion of casein and whey proteins. In breast milk, this proportion is roughly 40/60, sometimes 20/80. Most formula contains protein proportions that are roughly the same, at least according to the labels. But it's not a certainty that these proteins – after being heated – reach the baby's blood in similar proportions.

Carbohydrates Lactose is the most prevalent source of carbohydrates in formula. Some brands add maltodextrin, a corn sugar.

Vitamins The levels of vitamins and minerals are the same in all baby formula – they are mandated by law.

Milk base In the old days, if a father didn't have money to hire a wet nurse and his wife wasn't capable of breastfeeding the child, the baby had to make do with the milk of whatever lactating mammal happened to be available. Goats and cows were obvious choices, but donkeys were popular for this purpose too, and in fact donkey's milk turns out to be the closest in composition to the milk produced by a woman. These days, the "base" of almost all baby formula is cow's milk, given its wide availability. The industrial production of formula started about a hundred years ago.

Stomach cramps Because a baby's alimentary canal has to get used to food, almost all babies have stomach cramps at one time or another. Experimenting with special food is likely to be unnecessary. Stomach cramps are a fact of life for infants.

Second-stage formula The need for nutrients rises after about half a year – in particular, the baby needs extra protein, calcium, and iron. Many babies get this from the introduction of solid foods. Some manufacturers offer an enriched form of formula for bottle-fed babies who are six months and older. If your partner breastfeeds the child, you can leave this product on the shelf. All nutrients are administered through the extra food that you start at this time.

Special formula

Soy Only choose soy formula on the recommendation of a pediatrician or other medical professional. If your baby is allergic to cow's milk, soy doesn't necessarily help – roughly half the children who don't tolerate cow's milk very well have a similar reaction to soy milk.

Lactose-free formula This formula can work if your child has symptoms pointing to lactose intolerance, such as gassiness, diarrhea, diaper rash, and stomach cramps. In rare cases – 1 in 65,000 – the baby lacks the enzyme to process milk. Then, too, lactose-free formula is a good alternative. The lactose in this food has been replaced with another sugar, usually corn syrup or sucrose. The proportion of proteins and fats is identical to that of regular formula.

Hypoallergenic formula Recommended for babies who are hypersensitive to any number of proteins normally present in standard formula. In hypoallergenic formula, the coagulants of casein and whey proteins have been reduced and made as digestible as possible. Unfortunately, this doesn't exactly improve taste: the addition of sweeteners notwithstanding, hypoallergenic formula has a bitter and salty taste (it contains 30 to 90 per cent more salt than regular formula). Also, the manufacturing process reduces lactose, which manufacturers compensate for by adding carbohydrates like corn syrup, sucrose, and sometimes tapioca. Use only if recommended by a doctor.

Packaging Small cartons contain ready-to-use milk for one feeding. They can come in handy on the road but tend to be expensive. There are also bags and cans of concentrated powder that's added to warm water. Some cans have interior compartments, each containing enough powder for one feeding. Bring a flask of sterilized hot water, and you and the baby are ready for an outing.

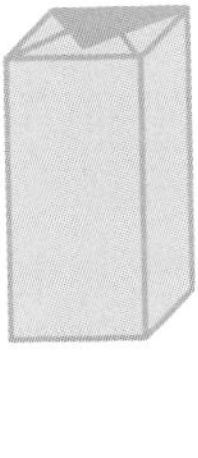

Shaken, not stirred!

You'll need some general beverage knowledge, practical and social skills, and patience with demanding customers. Practical necessities: bottle, nipple, measuring spoon, fresh milk powder, bottle warmer.

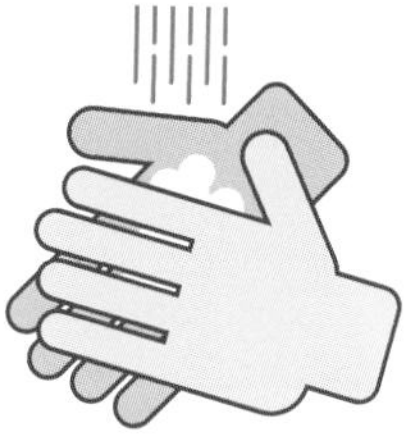

Do this:

- Wash your hands.
- Prepare water at the appropriate temperature (consult the packaging, or your healthcare provider, for guidance about whether you need to boil the water first and allow it to cool).
- Pour the water in the bottle.
- Add the powder. How much powder to how much water is indicated on the packaging.

- Fasten the nipple onto the top of the bottle, pinch the rubber protuberance between thumb and forefinger, and … *shake the bottle!* Continue until the powder is completely dissolved. Try not to create foam – foam affects the taste.
- Check the temperature. Dab a few drops onto your wrist. The milk can be a tad above body temperature. If it's too hot, hold the bottle briefly under cold running water.
- Sterilize both the bottle and the nipple after each use.

Hitting the bottle

- Warm the nipple under hot water until it's approximately at body temperature.
- Position the baby in your lap so that the head rests comfortably in the crook of your elbow. Hold up the head just a bit, making sure that it's in line with the body.

- Activate the baby's mouth reflex by stroking your finger across his cheek. He will turn his head and open his mouth.

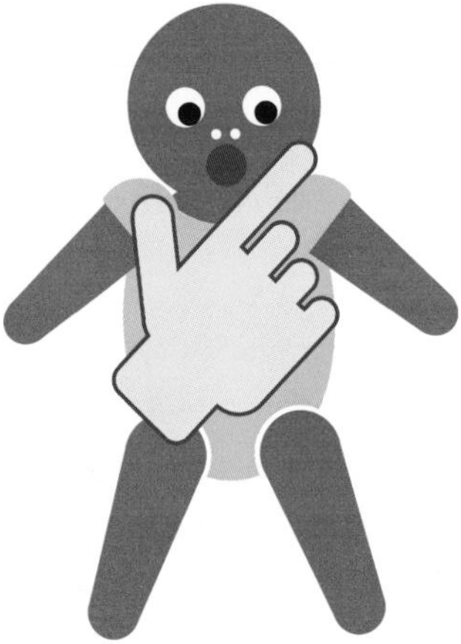

- Place the nipple in the mouth, aiming at the soft palate. See to it that he closes his lips around the entire perimeter of the teat.

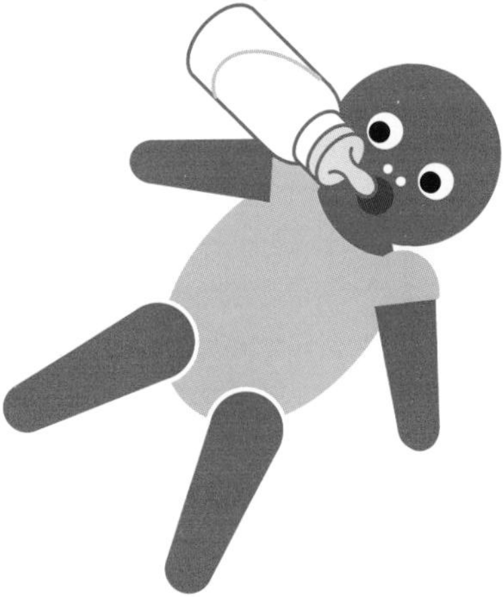

- Hold the bottle a bit askew, so that the milk fills the nipple. Don't let extra air into the bottle.

- Stop the feeding after 5 to 10 minutes. Lift the baby toward your chest, and gently stroke and pat his back in a circular motion. Keep at it for a couple of minutes; this allows the child to burp out the air he took in during the feeding. A breastfed baby may also burp.
- Resume feeding until the baby stops drinking. Don't pressure him to finish the whole bottle. Allow him to suck on the nipple even if he takes in no additional food. Burp the baby again.

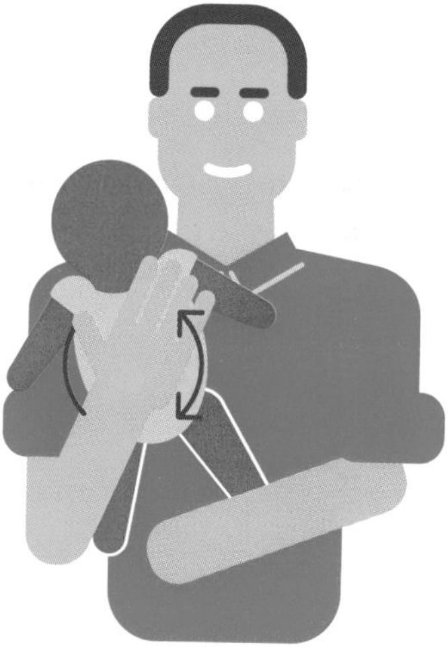

!

- Because the valve that closes the stomach is not entirely functional yet, some milk may come back out. Because milk flows quickly from a bottle, many infants drink more than they can handle.
- The bottle's milk stream can be too limited, depending on the size of the holes in the tip of the nipple. The holes are too small if the baby sucks in his cheeks; if the baby spits out the milk or is having a hard time swallowing mouthfuls of the beverage, that points to the opposite problem. You can check to see if the nipple is working properly by holding the bottle upside down. The milk is supposed to leak out at a rate of a few drops per second.
- Always discard any formula that the baby didn't drink.

Introducing solid food

Until he's about six months old, the average product needs nothing but mother's milk. Around that age, the product is ready for other foods.

Starting solids

When the mother decides to introduce solids, the weaning phase begins. It's a process with clear biological consequences regulated by supply and demand; when the breastfeeding frequency goes down, the production of breast milk goes down proportionally as well, although babies can and should continue to breastfeed after starting solids.

Serving extra food

Needed: plastic spoon (**1**), not too big for the baby's mouth; robust bowl (**2**), bib (**3**) and a stable child seat (**4**), that doesn't allow the baby too much room to move. Start with one extra (solid) meal per day. Don't take these initial extra feedings too seriously; they're really just exercises. For the first few months after the introduction of the extra food, breast milk or formula remains the baby's most important fuel.

The basic principles for introducing the extra food are simple:

- Start with vegetables or fruit.
- Slowly up the consistency, from smooth puréed food to chunkier iterations, from mashed with a fork to "normal."
- Gradually raise the fiber content; go from processed bread to wholewheat or multigrain.

Do as follows:

1. Prepare and heat the food.
2. Position the baby upright and put on his bib.
3. Fill the spoon about halfway with the food and gently push it against the child's lips. The baby might react by sticking out his tongue in an effort to suck on the food.
4. Keep repeating.
5. Be patient and encouraging.
6. Ensure that the food stays warm. Check the temperature a few times during the meal.

Preparing solid foods

Because the child can't yet chew food, you have to make it easy to swallow and digest. In the olden days, mom or dad often put the food into their own mouths, chewed it until it was smooth, then transferred it to the baby with a "food kiss". This is still common practice in many developing countries. We prefer kitchen equipment such as blenders.

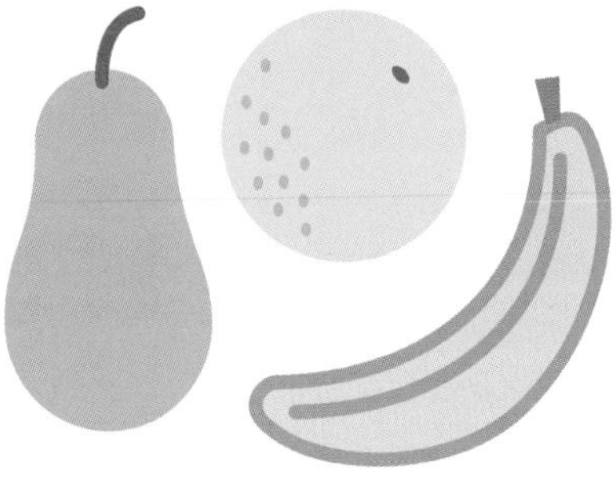

Fruit

Mash a piece of fruit with a fork. Then follow steps 2 through 5 on p107. Start with a pear or a banana and take it from there. Easy on the plums and prunes.

Vegetables

Boil until tender and purée until smooth. Follow steps 2 through 6 on p107. Start with cauliflower, carrots, or potatoes and expand the diet slowly. Easy on the cabbages.

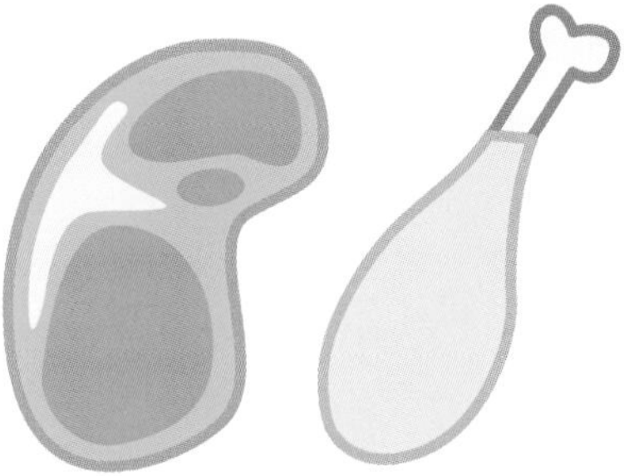

Meat and poultry

Cook the meat until well done, and purée it. Then follow steps 2 through 6 on p107. Chicken, beef, lamb and pork are all suitable for your baby.

Fish

Prepare until done, and purée. Then follow steps 2 through 6 on p107. Both white fish (such as cod or haddock) and "fatty" fish (salmon, tuna) are suitable. Remove all fish bones!

Snacks

Between meals, give the child a piece of bread or a cracker. Low salt snacks are best.

!

- Starting in month 9, you should purée the food a little less, to induce chewing.
- Introduce your child to only one new food at a time. Write down his reaction so that you can track what he may be allergic to.
- Don't put the spoon into your own mouth.

Input-related facts for Baby Managers

- Whether or not a woman should breastfeed the baby herself is a question as old as men's fears that the breasts will lose their firmness – we're talking **old**. In Europe's upper circles, from ancient times until the beginning of the 20th century, it was customary to have newborns fed by a wet nurse. A young Roman father would go to market and buy a visibly pregnant female slave; a 17th-century Parisian patrician would choose a sturdy country woman for the same purpose. A child might not see its parents again until it turned 3, when it was allowed to return from its stay with the wet nurse. Wet nurses were expected to follow a strict diet (soft lamb was a staple), to live a life of strict self-discipline (regular hours were considered key), and to perform special exercises to keep their breasts in top condition.
- A growth spurt occurs when your baby enters a new stage of physiological development, and his feeding rhythm changes right along with it. This often results in fussiness and crying. The baby refuses to eat or may want to eat constantly, to increase the milk supply.
- When milk production starts, your partner may experience "engorgement," where expulsion of the milk is unsuccessful. Show her plenty of understanding and keep handing her cold washcloths to relieve the pain. Or, more practical still, keep giving her the baby; feeding often works wonders.
- If the mother is tense, cold, or in pain, the milk-ejection reflex (or let-down) may not occur. It usually returns when she relaxes (a breast massage, a hot shower, or a warm drink might help). The let-down is not just triggered by the baby's suckling on the breast. If the mother hears the child cry, or merely thinks about him, milk may trickle from her breasts.
- There is a likely relationship between the lack of cholesterol in baby formula and a grown-up's cholesterol level. Because there is

hardly any cholesterol in formula, the body is forced to produce it on its own. This "tuning" of the body can lead to higher cholesterol levels later in life. This means that adults who were breastfed as children are thought to have generally lower cholesterol levels.

- After delivery, almost all mothers are capable of breastfeeding (only about two per cent have physical ailments that thwart the production of milk). Although organizations such as Unicef, the WHO and the American Academy of Pediatrics recommend nothing but breast milk for at least six months, about 1 out of 5 American mothers chooses formula from day one. Overall, the incidence of initial breastfeeding is on the rise – but in the U.S., as in most western countries, the percentage of moms still breastfeeding after six months is down to about 20 per cent. Swedish women, thanks in part to their lavish maternity leave arrangements, rank among the western world's best breastfeeders. Ninety-eight per cent start off after birth, and 6 months later, 53 per cent still serve baby's favorite. If children are allowed to breastfeed as long as they like, most stop around age 3 or 4. However, your partner might run into problems if she's planning to continue breastfeeding past toddlerhood. In 2001, an Illinois (U.S.) mother made headlines after a judge ruled that she was to be separated from her then 5-year-old son because continued breastfeeding had supposedly created a situation with "enormous potential harm to this child". Seven months later, the child was allowed to return home, on the condition that the mother would take parenting courses and counseling. Such extreme judgments aside, there is no basis for any age limit to breastfeeding other than the child's preference.
- The ancient warm-water method is best, but if you keep a cool head you can warm mother's milk in the microwave. Foods tend to heat unevenly in the microwave and the outside of a bottle may be cooler than the liquid inside. Check the temperature carefully before serving.

Output

5

Output

Workspace

To deal with your product's output, an efficient workspace is key. If you're handy, you can make such a workstation yourself (being the slightly squeamish sort, we prefer "workstation" to "changing table") or buy a manufactured one. They come in all kinds of shapes and sizes, from clip-on table extenders and integrated models featuring both a pad and a baby bath, to classic pieces of furniture that will dominate the room.

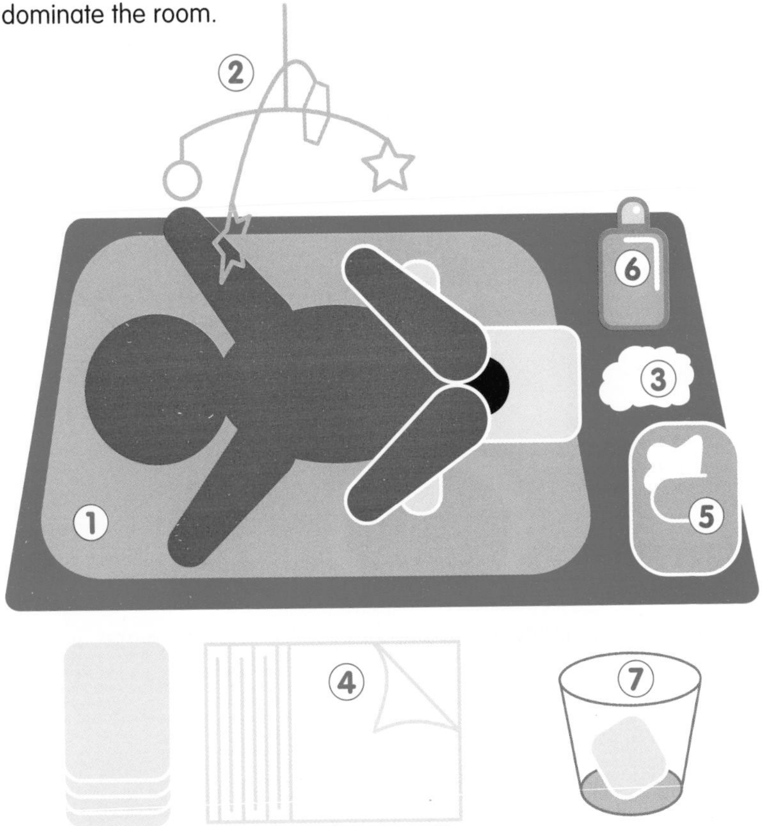

Dimensions

Choose a work surface that's at least 30 inches wide and 22 inches deep, and that's between 36 and 42 inches in height. Make sure it extends an inch or so toward the front, so you'll have a place for your toes.

Safety

A safe workstation has smooth edges and doesn't tilt or wobble, not even when its doors or drawers are open. The back and sides should have an elevated edge. Keep it away from radiators, and make sure there are no furnishings around for the baby to grab on to, such as knobs, handles, hooks, or curtain cords. Never leave the child alone on the work surface.

Materials

Cover most of the work surface with a thick pad (1), preferably the kind with raised edges. Hang a mobile over it to distract the baby (2). Keep the following materials within reach: moist baby wipes (use only after the baby is at least a month old: these wipes tend to contain alcohol that could dry out a newborn's skin); cotton balls (3); thin cotton towels (4); diaper wipes or wash cloths (5); baby oil or cream (6); and a generous supply of diapers. You'll be going through about 4,500 diapers in the child's early years. Sorry about that. Use a diaper pail (7) to temporarily dispose of used diapers. The odor of diaper pails can be somewhat neutralized by a deodorant; some fancy models automatically wrap the diaper in a germ-killing plastic bag.

Output containment

Your product's tangible output should be guided into a soft, flexible shell that you secure around the baby's nether regions. You can choose between cloth diapers and disposable ones.

Disposable diaper

One-piece solution made from wood pulp, chemicals and oil products. Some are suitable for bathing/swimming. All are guaranteed to get wet on the inside. But you knew that.

Cotton diaper

Available in different configurations: a 2-piece number with cloth and pants, or an all-in-one solution that can be a square piece of fabric or a pre-shaped one. The following table can help you choose which one's right for you:

Disposable diaper	Cotton diaper
• Expensive	• Cost 25-50% less
• Easy to install and remove	• Typically requires more steps, and requires doing laundry
• Single-use only, taxes the environment	• Use over and over: lower burden on the environment
• Holds feces and bacteria, ends up in household trash/landfills	• Feces are rinsed away in toilet, end up in sewer system
• Contains traces of dioxine, long-term health risks unclear	• Bleached cotton contains dioxine traces; unbleached eco-version
• Higher environmental burden during manufacture	• Production involves pesticides and chemicals, but eco-cotton doesn't
• Contains sodium polyacrylate, an absorbant	• No link to asthma
• Possible link between disposable diapers and asthma due to ephemeral gases produced by material	• More likely to lead to earlier success with potty training
• Can slow down success of potty training	

Disposal

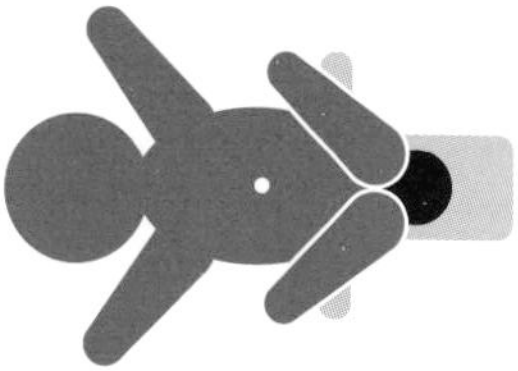

Remove your baby's output as follows:

1. Wash your hands.

2. Prepare the necessary materials. Take a wash cloth moistened in warm water that's been allowed to cool to approximate body temperature. Or go for the convenience of special pre-moistened baby wipes. Do not use soap!

3. Put the baby on the workstation surface, on the back, and pull back the diaper.

4. If the diaper is only wet, move on to step 8.

5. Gently grab the baby's feet and pull them up.

6. If it's a boy, wipe upwards. If it's a girl, wipe downwards, reducing the chance of vaginal infection. Do not touch (open) the labia.

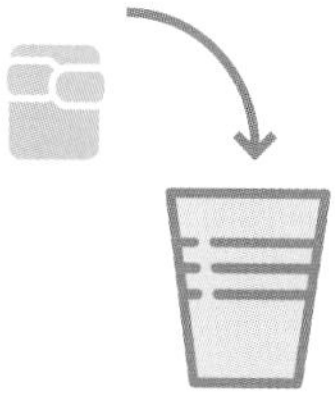

7. Dispose of the diaper.

8. Clean the area with a soft washcloth soaked in warm water. Use a clean one for every diaper change.

9. Dry the skin folds, the insides of the thighs, and the buttocks, using a breeze generated by a towel, or a hairdryer (don't set the dryer to "heat," just to "blow").

10. Open the new diaper completely and place it under your baby with the closure tabs facing up at you.

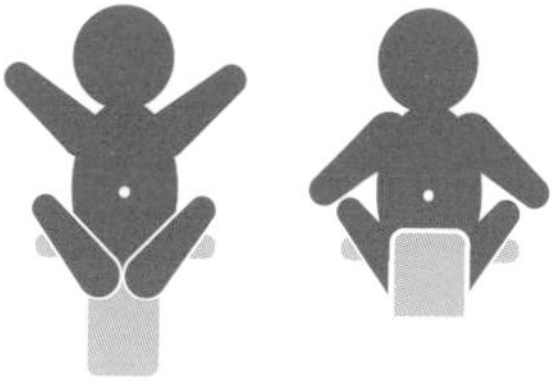

11. Center the baby on the diaper.

12. Fold the front of the diaper over the baby's genitals. If it's a boy, let the penis fall forward.

13. Fasten the side flaps.

14. Ensure that you can slide 1 or 2 fingers between the diaper and the baby's belly. Don't let the diaper cover the navel stump.

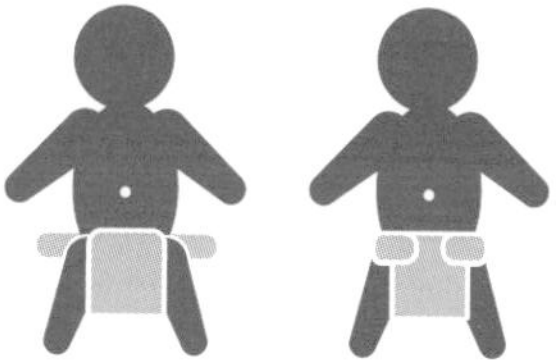

Output statistics Frequency, color, weight, and composition of the output are important indicators of how well your product is functioning.
Time The output is stimulated by the intestinal reflex. Filling the stomach invokes a slowly pulsing motion in the larger intestine. Most babies produce feces several times a day, but some do so after every feeding while others (especially when breastfeeding) don't have a bowel movement for 1 or 2 days or even longer. Babies expel urine about 15 times a day. If a baby produces fewer than 4 or 5 wet diapers a day, he's probably not drinking enough.
Color The first days after the birth the color of the output ranges from dark green to black. The primary feces, called meconium, consists of slime and cells from the intestinal membrane that have accumulated in the digestive tract during the assembly process. The dark color is the result of bile production. The thick, sticky, hard-to-remove meconium is often expelled during or shortly after the birth and is sometimes found in the amniotic fluid – sometimes indicating fetal distress. Within days the baby switches to easier-to-handle waste disposal functions. Depending on the nourishment provided, the color will change to mustardy-yellow (breast milk) or brown (formula). Other foods, down the line, contribute to different shades and colors.
Composition The output of breastfed babies is a semi-solid paste. Formula usually leads to a creamier consistency. Lumps in the feces can indicate a digestive disturbance; thin, unusually odorous feces may point to an infection; and a slimy output coupled with diarrhea may be an indicator of irritated bowels. Blood in the diaper is usually caused by small tears in the anus that may be the result of hard stools. See your pediatrician.

After you've started feeding your baby solid foods, his feces may contain undigested chunks.

Output-related facts for Baby Managers

- Diaper rash is a skin affliction consisting of redness and small bumps and even sores around the baby's genitals and anus. The rash is caused by bacteria that form ammonia in a chemical reaction with urine. You can treat this with frequent diaper changes (every 2 to 3 hours) and by gently applying a zinc ointment. Disposable diapers seem to cause more frequent rashes than cotton ones. See your doctor if the problems persist.
- A clean diaper is not as innocent as it looks. The blinding white color of a disposable diaper is the result of an intensive bleach and softening process that has dioxine as a byproduct. A diaper's extreme absorption capabilities are possible thanks to a polymer called sodium polyacrylate. This toxic substance (known to cause heart failure and death when injected into lab rats) can stick to a baby's genitals and cause allergic reactions. In many countries, sodium polyacrylate has been banned from tampons. The germ-killing properties of a diaper are partly the work of TBT (tributylin), which the World Health Organization considers to be one of the most harmful substances present in consumer products. Even in low concentrations, TBT can influence a child's immune system and hormonal balance. Some researchers and scientists see a direct link between these substances in diapers, and the asthma problems that have been rising for decades, especially among children. In 1999, a much-debated experiment was carried out in which lab mice were exposed, in close quarters, to four named-brand diapers – three disposables and a cotton specimen. One of the diapers oozed enough nasty chemicals for the test animals to develop irritated eyes, noses, and throats, in a few cases severe enough to be likened to an

asthma attack. The gases leaching from that diaper contained toluene, xylene, ethyl benzene, and styrene. The cotton diaper, one of the "regular" disposable diapers and an eco-friendly version did not induce breathing difficulties. Toxicologists use mice because the symptoms displayed by the animals are likely to occur in humans, too. The researchers say that additional analysis is needed to determine whether there is indeed a link between wearing disposable diapers and breathing difficulties. (Not to alarm you, but residual amounts of toxic substances are found in a great number of consumer products – everything from sports jerseys and bandaids to maxi pads and blow-up toys made of soft, pliable plastic.)

- A different study, carried out in 2000 by the University of Kiel in Germany, also revealed the white disposable diaper to be a problematic product. A team of doctors suggested that male infertility – a phenomenon that's been on the rise in recent years – can perhaps be attributed to the wearing of disposable diapers. These products tend to keep the temperature of the scrotum about one degree higher than the temperature of the body; boys who wore cotton diapers showed a considerably lower increase. The testicular temperature should ideally be *lower* than the body temperature. It's true that sperm-producing cells are inactive during the baby's first two years, but the normal development of these cells requires the temperature that nature intended. The Kiel researchers, too, urge follow-up studies. Health authorities generally deny that disposable diapers are risky for babies. However, if you want to be on the safe side, cotton diapers are the way to go.

Marketing

6

Marketing

Size and characteristics of the market

You will be launching your product in a market that is characterized by heavy competition and boundless growth.

Market analysis

Your product is hardly unique. Between 50,000 BC – when *homo sapiens* came on the scene – and 1955, about 100 billion babies were launched. The current population of the world represents 6 per cent of the total number of humans who ever lived. The challenge is to determine your possible competitive advantage in this ancient but very dynamic market. The key to doing that is the TFR or total fertility rate – which is the number of babies that the average woman delivers. A TFR of 2.1 is seen as the "replacement" number, meaning that, discounting big shifts in migration patterns, the population will remain stable if women produce, on average, 2.1 babies. If the TFR is higher than 2.1, your product's competitors become more plentiful; wherever the TFR is lower, the competition diminishes. Here's the TFR prognosis for the world market:

Region	1990	2000	2010	2025	
World	3.4	2.8	2.5	2.3	(TFR)
Developing countries	4.7	3.1	2.7	2.4	
Developed countries	1.9	1.6	1.7	1.7	

Source: United Nations Population Division and U.S. Census Bureau

This table shows that the number of children will decline all over the world; your product's competitive advantage is looking quite good. Although the TFR in many developing countries is still on the high side, it is expected to go down fast. The western world, however, leads the decline: of the 20 most developed countries, 19 rate below the replacement level, including Japan and most well-off European countries. The United States stands at 2.1 exactly.

Global competition

Still, worldwide competition will remain fierce. Every second brings around 4 new babies, or 79 million newborns per year. The global population rises 1.19 per cent annually. The total number of people is expected to rise from 7 billion now to nearly 9 billion by 2042. The countries where the rise is starkest are Liberia (4.5 per cent annually), Burundi (3.9 per cent), Afghanistan (3.8 per cent), Western Sahara (3.7 per cent) and East Timor (3.5 per cent). Experts expect an end to population growth by the end of the century. Peak population will occur between 2050 and 2075.

U.S. competition

The market outlook for your product in the U.S. is challenging, to say the least. That is to say, competition abounds. Population growth in the U.S. is the highest in the developed world. Total population is projected to reach 439 million by 2050, a 44 per cent increase from 2008. The biggest driver is immigration, but with more than 4 million newborns a year, babies make for their own impressive boom. The birth rate (childbirths per 1,000 people per year) is on the rise, having increased from 14.14 in 2003 to an estimated 14.18 in 2008.

European competition

Europe is a dream market for the ambitious baby manager. In some European countries, you can almost stop working as long as you keep on making babies. In the EU, the TFR number is currently at 1.48, with birth rates slowly dropping from 10.2 in 2004 to an estimated 9.97 in 2008. There are indications that the number will go up somewhat, but not enough for the population to increase. By around 2025, the total number of inhabitants in the 27 countries of the European Union will be 470 million. It is expected that, by the end of the century, 45 per cent of western Europeans will be 60 years old or older. Germany tries to prevent the specter of walkers crowding strollers off the sidewalks by rewarding parents with a bonus of $30,000 for each newborn. The French, for their part, receive a generous tax break and other financial benefits. Spain, Italy, and Poland also reward young parents financially. In Russia, every second baby is greeted with a windfall of $12,000. Generous bonuses and affordable, ever-improving childcare arrangements make Europe a fertile market for product development.

Other markets

Since 2004, Australia, with its immense territory and its population of just 21 million, has been rewarding young parents with a bonus of $5,000 per baby, perhaps leading to the TFR increase from 1.77 in 2004 to a current 1.81. In Japan, where the birth rate has dropped dramatically from 9.61 (2003) to an estimated 7.87 (2008), parents can count on being pampered with baby bonuses in the form of everything from cell phones to hard cash.

Warning All products, children not excluded, thrive on competition, the heartbeat of evolution. When competing with each other, children learn to manage stress, success and disappointment, develop patience and perseverance, learn responsibility, and figure out how to set and achieve goals. Developing your product in a country where there's less rivalry might seem attractive, but keep the risks in mind. Kids might be pampered, smothered even, by excessive (state) attention – and possibly they'll have septuagenarians as playmates.

Target audience

Planning is key. Don't wait until your baby is suddenly there; prepare your market for the change ahead. Who's your target audience? In fact, you have several.

- **Partner** Invest in a relationship with her. She is of critical importance to the baby's development. See to it that, between the two of you, your tasks and ambitions are mutually understood and agreed upon.
- **Employer** The presence of the baby will test relationships at work with colleagues and bosses. Should your product malfunction or perform sub-optimally, you may be called home. Also, your financial burden is bound to get heavier. Make sure that everyone understands that you won't shirk your professional duties but that you'd appreciate their flexibility if home-front eventualities occur.

- **Family** When your product requires extra care and attention, you know you can fall back on these volunteers. A pleasant working relationship with parents and in-laws can save you lots of headaches. Clamp down early on unfair competition from your siblings (and those of your partner).

- **Neighbors** Mentally screen those around you for potential babysitting duties. Even if you wouldn't dream of entrusting your product to these people, be courteous and alert them to coming changes, from fewer parking spaces due to visits by fawning friends and family, to noise issues caused by your baby.
- **Friends** Prevent damage to friendships, or their loss, by:
  - making clear arrangements and schedules covering

domestic and baby-related tasks: this lets you know when you're free to see your friends.
- going out (or hanging out) with several friends at the same time.
- organizing a weekly friends' night at your place, an evening when everyone is welcome.

• **Babysitter** A reliable and caring babysitter is your key to freedom. Find one early!

Childcare

Depending on your budget, your childcare options are abundant or meager. In most countries, desirable daycare centers have waiting lists. Explore the possibilities well ahead of the baby's arrival:

Au pair

If you have a spare bedroom, consider hiring a live-in au pair. You'll owe this person a roof over her head ("her" because most likely it's a young woman), meals, a modest salary or allowance, and, depending on your country and jurisdiction, you might have to pay for health insurance and other coverage. Virtually every country has dedicated au pair agencies that can provide detailed information and help make the best possible match.

Home daycare

With 3 or 4 other children, your son or daughter becomes a guest in the home of another mother and/or father who specializes in providing childcare. Ask for referrals. If your country's authorities require a permit or certification for these small-scale operations, ask to see it.

Governess/nanny

The luxury version of the au pair. This professional and experienced childcare provider can take over parental duties at a moment's notice.

Parent-participation daycare

This is a privately organized, self-governing group of parents that take care of the kids collectively, usually taking turns. There is no paid leadership, no certification, and the rules are whatever the adults involved agree they should be.

Professional daycare center

Your child is assigned to a class that meets daily in a special facility, not unlike a school. Care is provided by professional, certified childcare specialists. You can often choose from full-day care (morning and afternoon) or partial care. Daycare centers tend to be booked long in advance, so get your application in as soon as you learn of the pregnancy.

Costs of childcare

After the mortgage, childcare is the biggest expense in most family budgets, unless you're lucky enough to live in a Scandinavian country where childcare is a fully state-sponsored expense. But if you're enjoying a milder climate and less horrific tax bills, childcare can easily burn a hole in your wallet.

Most countries do provide subsidies, depending on income level and prevalent ideas about working women. In ageing Europe, subsidized childcare has risen sharply over the past few years as society needs more women to step into the workforce fulltime. In the U.S., childcare support can be provided by employers; state-level support is only available to low-income families.

If you can't afford a Mary Poppins, or want to cut down on daycare expenses, consider these tips:

- **Make it mobile** I happen to be writing this in the car, waiting for my daughter to finish her swimming practice. If your work allows it, go wireless and you can work anywhere.
- **Share the care** Share a nanny or another caregiver with two (or more) families who have children of similar ages. Hit the internet for bulletin boards and forums on this topic.
- **Share the care part II** Turn the babysitting co-op principle into do-it-yourself daycare. Get together with other parents of young children and take turns in taking care of the kids. There is no paid leadership, no certification, and the rules are whatever the adults involved agree they should be. Find guidelines on the web.
- **Work in shifts** If your partner takes the early shift and you do the late shift, there's less need for back-up care. (Dis)advantage: you'll see your wife even less.
- **Bring your baby to work** Since he is your number one teacher in management skills, it's no more than fair: your baby deserves a suitable space at the office. Your colleagues might need some

time to appreciate the teachings of this inimitable management guru. Seriously, there are lots of companies and public agencies that have created childcare facilities. To set an example, Dutch parliament offers a crèche to its members. If you're not a Dutch politician and your company has no daycare center yet, be a revolutionary and persuade your boss.

- **Move next-door to your parents** A truly old-fashioned tip, but awesomely handy if you get along. Convince your parents to postpone their cruise plans until your kids reach school age.

Effects on your child

What effect does "third-party" daycare have on the development of your child? That's a hot topic in developmental psychology. An ongoing American study, conducted by the National Institute of Child Health and Human Development's Study of Early Child Care, which follows 1,300 children, feeds the discussion. The debate started when the researchers presented preliminary results in 2001 that concluded that daycare is a risk factor for some children. Kids who spent more than 30 hours a week in daycare were said to be more likely to display aggressive and aberrant behavior. This was explained by saying that in daycare centers, young children's brains might have received a surfeit of stimuli. But that conclusion drew heavy fire. Despite the size of the sample group, critics point out that the results are compiled based on hard-to-quantify observations, and that there is no control-group data from children who were predominantly cared for at home, by their parents.

Still, the conclusions resonate elsewhere too. A Dutch professor of developmental psychology, Marianne Riksen-Walraven, has often pointed out that daycare may have a problematic effect on children. The sheer scale on which childcare is now being farmed out to professionals is an "evolutionary first", she says. In other words: the long-term consequences are unknown. The Early Child Care study does offer some new insights as researchers continue tracking the development of the same children. In 2005, a new report found that by third grade, those who had spent long hours in childcare continued to score higher in math and reading skills, and that their higher likelihood of aggressive behavior had vanished. But it also showed that their poor work habits and social skills still needed improvement.

! While the jury is still out, there is little reason to fret about the effects of daycare on your child. Observe his reactions when he's there and see if you find cause for concern. And, especially with very young children, try to put them in daycare only for as many days as is strictly necessary.

Choosing a daycare center

Visit several daycare facilities and choose wisely. Pay special attention to these factors:

- **Contact**: Do the childcare providers seem to enjoy being around the children? Do they have eye-level contact with their charges?
- **Space**: Are there plenty of toys and educational materials? Is it safe, tidy, and organized?
- **Atmosphere**: Do the children sound and look happy and involved in the activities? Do the childcare workers' voices and body language reflect patience, contentment, fulfillment?
- **Child/staff ratio**: How many children are there to a group or class? How many childcare professionals are there to how many children?
- **Experience**: If possible, scrutinize the backgrounds and experience

levels of the staff. How many of the childcare workers are certified, and how many are apprenticing/interning?

- **Are there any men on staff?** It's unlikely: childcare is almost exclusively a female-run operation. This might lead to girls' norms being the dominant ones, so that working with clay or play-doh means making pretty figurines instead of seeing whether the material sticks to the ceiling when you throw it heavenwards with enough force. Boys are falling behind in school in ever-growing numbers. They're 10 times as likely as girls to display hyperactivity, 3 times as likely to be sent to "special" schools for kids with learning disabilities, and more likely to be made to repeat a class. Also, they're more often dyslexic, more likely to stutter... Many experts see this as the result of a heavily feminized kindergarten and elementary-school culture. Some writers even speak of a "war against boys". This discussion is much older than it may seem. Especially in countries where primary education has been feminized for a long time – between 1900 and 1910 the percentage of female teachers in U.S. and the U.K. was already at 80 and 75 per cent respectively – critics warned of *The Woman Peril*, as an eagerly-quoted book was called. The menace supposedly created "a feminized manhood, emotional, illogical, non-combative against public evils". In France, Pierre de Coubertin responded to this movement with his call to revive the Olympic Games and, in England, Robert Baden-Powell wrote his *Scouting for Boys*, a guidebook for the toughening of lads that can read like the precursor to Con and Hal Iggulden's 2007 *The Dangerous Book for Boys*. Interestingly, evidence for the assumption that female teachers have a negative effect on the development of boys is surprisingly thin, even absent. A recent large-scale study carried out in the Netherlands, involving 5,181 grade eight pupils, 251 teachers and 163 schools, did not establish any relation between the gender of the teacher and the achievement, attitude and behavior of children. Nevertheless, if you have a son, you may want to rejoice if you find a suitable daycare center that employs a man.

More info: childcareaware.org – Great info hub for info on all aspects of childcare, including a glossary of common childcare terms.

Brand name

Spend ample time on determining your brand strategy. The brand name you give your product has to last throughout its life cycle.

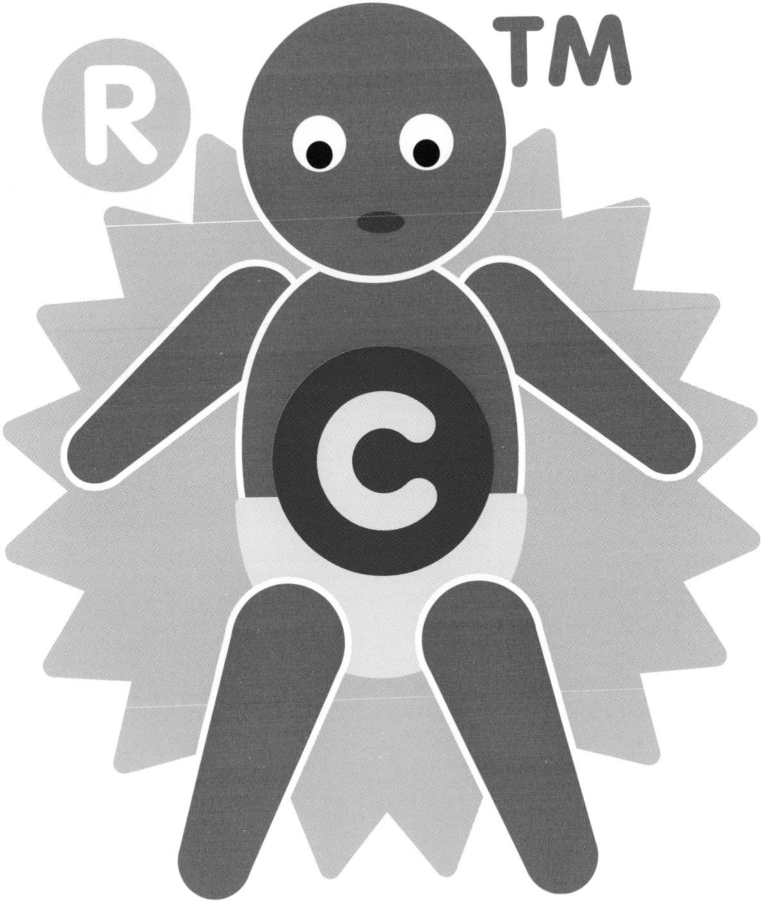

Family name

You can give your child your own family name or that of your partner. In most countries, that's a once-and-for-all choice that also applies to all subsequent children. About 5 per cent of all newborns receive their mothers' last names.

Given name

- Don't choose a name where the sound of the last vowel is the same as the sound of the first vowel in the last name (Peter Terwilliger, Patrick Dickson).
- A longish given name often combines well with a short last name, and vice versa.
- If you have a common family name, give your child a more unusual first one – but don't forget, it's got to be userfriendly, too!
- If you'll be launching multiple products, choose different initials for each one, and check that the combination of initials doesn't carry unintended double entendres or undesirable associations.
- Consider adding a special meaning to your product's brand name. At sites like **behindthename.com** and **wiki.name.com** you can check out the etymology and history of given names.

Legal stipulations

These vary by country. In the U.S. you can name your kid Toyota, Teflon, Just Trouble – almost whatever you like. But officialdom in some nations may not deem your chosen name legally appropriate. If the civil servant who registers your baby considers himself the arbiter of taste, nixes your chosen given name, and can't get you to reconsider, he (or she) may be authorized to officially substitute a more "suitable" name. In that case, your only recourse would be to start legal proceedings to force the authorities to accept the name you want to give your child.

Most popular brand names

	1942	2006	2007	2008	2009	2010	2011
1.	Mary	Emily	Emily	Emma	Isabella	Isabella	Sophia
2.	Barbara	Emma	Isabella	Isabella	Emma	Sophia	Isabella
3.	Patricia	Madison	Emma	Emily	Olivia	Emma	Emma
4.	Linda	Isabella	Ava	Olivia	Sophia	Olivia	Olivia
5.	Carol	Ava	Madison	Ava	Ava	Ava	Ava
6.	Sandra	Abigail	Sophia	Madison	Emily	Emily	Emily
7.	Judith	Olivia	Olivia	Sophia	Madison	Abigail	Abigail
8.	Nancy	Hannah	Abigail	Abigail	Abigail	Madison	Madison
9.	Betty	Sophia	Hannah	Elizabeth	Chloe	Chloe	Mia
10.	Carolyn	Samantha	Elizabeth	Chloe	Mia	Mia	Chloe

	1942	2006	2007	2008	2009	2010	2011
1.	James	Jacob	Jacob	Jacob	Jacob	Jacob	Jacob
2.	Robert	Michael	Michael	Michael	Ethan	Ethan	Mason
3.	John	Joshua	Ethan	Ethan	Michael	Michael	William
4.	William	Ethan	Joshua	Joshua	Alexander	Jayden	Jayden
5.	Richard	Matthew	Daniel	Daniel	William	William	Noah
6.	David	Daniel	Christopher	Alexander	Joshua	Alexander	Michael
7.	Charles	Andrew	Anthony	Anthony	Daniel	Noah	Ethan
8.	Thomas	Christopher	William	William	Jayden	Daniel	Alexander
9.	Ronald	Anthony	Matthew	Christopher	Noah	Aiden	Aiden
10.	Donald	William	Andrew	Matthew	Christopher	Anthony	Daniel

Source: US Social Security Administration

More info: The web is teeming with sites where you can find ideas for a suitable name, but the trophy for the best resource should go to Babynamewizard.com, where nothing less than the "art and science of baby names" is practised, including a Namipedia and a Namevoyager. Speaking of a unique brand name, I was happy to learn that even these self-proclaimed name scientists hadn't discovered my son's name, IJsbrand, yet. **All-babynames.com**, the runner-up in this category, also missed out on this first name that, I admit, hasn't been fashionable since 1576. I submitted the name to them so other parents with a knack for the antiquated might consider calling their boy "shimmering sword", which is the meaning of IJsbrand. I can't say yet whether IJsbrand himself will appreciate our choice.

PR and promotion

Here are the pillars of your PR strategy:

Direct mail Targeted action that enables you to share news of your product launch with selected addresses. Use e-mail or snail mail. If the latter, book a printer ahead of the delivery date.

Launch party Further brighten the product launch with festivities for your target group; invitations can be combined with the birth announcements. There are professional agencies that will organize the launch party for you, if you have too much on your mind already.

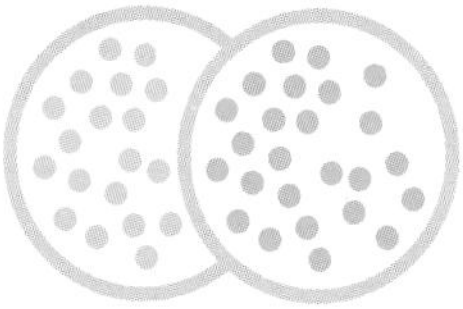

Website A baby manager worth his salt will like to blog about his brand new product. Needless to say, many websites enable you to start just such a blog, complete with a virtual photo album and uploadable video footage.

Communication

7

Communication

From receiver to transmitter

In the field of baby management, effective communication is the key to successful product development. Communicative skills such as play, speaking *parentese*, and offering consolation are all part of the baby manager's skill set.

Your product's communication tools

Crying

Your baby comes with a limited but effective way of communicating: making a terrible racket. The average baby cries for about an hour each day. There's almost always a cause for these crying spells. Here are the most common ones.

Cause	Solution
Discomfort	Change diaper, check if baby is too cold or too hot, see to it that clothing is comfortable and not too tight.
Hunger	Give him milk.
Irritation	Remove the source of irritation, such as excessive light or sound.
Stomach cramps	Burp the baby. Or put him on his back and move his legs as if he's cycling.
Loneliness	Physical contact should help.
Fatigue/ exhaustion	Relax the baby; feed him, bathe him, talk to him, rock him.
Illness	Consult a doctor if you notice anything out of the ordinary.

Research reveals that mothers can often recognize their own baby's sound shortly after birth. They can also distinguish different kinds of crying.

One in 10 babies is outfitted with a capacity for excessive crying. If your child cries at least 3 hours a day, 3 days a week, for 3 weeks or more, ask your pediatrician what can be done.

Talking

The word infant comes from the Latin *infans*, meaning "incapable of speaking". After about 2 months, this assessment begins to seem less apt; the baby may by now be sticking out his tongue and pursing his lips, while beginning to form soft sounds with his breath. The first vowels typically aren't far behind. They tend to be ohs and ahs. Consonants are next, and his vocabulary now includes sounds like da, ma, and ka. After roughly a year, you may hear the first deliberate monosyllabic word.

From transmitter to receiver

Providing comfort and a sense of security is a key aspect of the first stages of your communications strategy. You can achieve this feat by doing the following:

- **Little finger** Wash your hands. Moisten your pinkie finger and gently insert it into the baby's mouth to satisfy his suckling reflexes. When you do this, take care to turn the soft part of your finger to the front, so as not to damage the gums or the roof of the baby's mouth with your nail.
- **Movement** Your baby could be experiencing a kind of separation anxiety from the womb – a wish to be back in the only environment he's known for 9 months. To minimize discomfort and alienation, try to put him in a "prenatal" state of mind.
  - Hold the baby against your chest, roughly where your heart is, and softly rock him, either while you're sitting down or walking around.
  - Make or sing soft rhythmical sounds.
  - No dice? Put the baby in his pram, and go for a walk.
- **Pacifier** Like the little-finger technique, the pacifier creates, in the baby's mind, the illusion of suckling a breast. Pacifiers can be especially effective for babies who empty their bottle of formula fairly quickly. Using the pacifier generally prevents the baby from sucking on his thumb or fingers. Babies that do this might develop crooked teeth.
- **Nothing** If your child is not in pain, not hungry, and not in need of a diaper change, and yet he persists in protesting when you cradle him, don't panic. Most likely, fatigue is bothering him, and the problem will take care of itself when he sleeps.

! Your non-verbal communications are, for now, the baby's only cues. If you're tense, you can't help but create tension in the baby. If you're relaxed, however, the baby will soon chill too.

Other forms of communication

Tune your communications to the frequency of the receiver.

Talking

Repeat the sounds your baby makes. Tell the baby what you're doing from moment to moment. The sounds and words you employ to talk to your baby (high notes and simple, melodic sentences) are often called *motherese* or *parentese*. Speaking *parentese* has long been recommended as a way of stimulating the baby's language acquisition skills. Research on the matter is inconclusive, but it is clear that talking to the baby is of great importance to the child's development. Deaf babies prattle about as much during their first six months as hearing children do. After half a year, however, the development of their verbal communications comes to a halt, probably because they're not learning to mimic sounds.

Music

Music hastens a child's creative and intellectual development. Choose music with simple percussion and a single melody. Cradle the baby and dance him around the room while humming or singing along.

Reading

Reading to a baby stimulates the child's imagination, as well as his listening skills, his own capacity for reading, and his ability to focus his attention. Despite these advantages, many older children now read just a few minutes a day. If you want your child to like books, pull them out every day and read them to him.

Play

One of the paramount forms of communication between you and your product is the interaction that's fueled by play. What is the function of play?

In ancient Greek, the word paida means "game" or "play", and the word *paideia* (which shows up, for instance, in the English word "pedagogical" refers to bringing up children. "People learn through playing," Plato wrote. "Nothing is retained through forced education." After the decline of Greek civilization, such notions were unpopular for many centuries. Until well into the 18th century, play was thought of as a senseless waste of time. No longer. Since the beginning of the last century, scientists, philosophers and historians have all been analyzing the significance of play. Sigmund Freud thought that play enabled children to develop and hone problem-solving skills. U.S. paleontologist John E. Pfeiffer saw play as nothing less than the origin of art. His compatriot Brian Sutton-Smith, an education professor, found after a thorough study that play generates variations in behavior and thought. And the Dutch historian Johan Huizinga demonstrated in his classical study Homo Ludens that playing games is a staple of all aspects of human culture. His 1949 definition is still accepted and quoted by other academics:

> *"In summary, play is an act, undertaken in freedom, . . . that can fully occupy the player's consciousness, and for which there is no direct payoff in terms of usefulness or material gain; it takes place within deliberate limitations of time and space, and is subject to a certain orderliness as it is bound by rules . . ."*

Huizinga also noted that play creates "community cohesion".

Play as an engine

After a general consensus on the function and significance of play had been reached, the time came to determine what kinds of play befit a growing child. Swiss psychologist Jean Piaget established important notions in this field. He saw even young children as small researchers and scientists who discover through trial and error how the world around them functions. This process, Piaget believed, had several development phases. During the first two years of its life – the sensory-motor phase – the child learns to control bodily and physical reflexes. He will gradually become conscious of himself as a separate physical entity, surrounded by other separate physical objects and entities. Piaget's ideas culminated in a revision of the role of parents and teachers: they went from bestowers of skills and knowledge to gentle guides that enable children to navigate life's paths more or less independently. During this journey, the vehicle that propels the child from one major step to the next is play. Russian psychologist Lev Vigotsky (1896–1934), whose theory has gained much popular ground in recent years, even called play the engine of a child's development. He posited that children do not develop autonomously as much as through a process of imitation.

In the table below, you'll find a brief overview of the skills a young child acquires through play:

Play	Skills acquired
Finger play, hand play	Develops fine motor skills, language and arithmetic skills, coordination.
Fantasy and "pretend" play	Social skills, creative expression, language.
Puzzles and jigsaws	Abstract reasoning, spatial skills, understanding shapes.

Blocks	Promote a basic understanding of gravity, stability, weight, balance.
Sandbox	Geometry, problem-solving, motor skills.
Coloring, drawing, painting	Creativity, emotional expression, symbolic representation, fine motor skills.

Toys

Don't bother with expensive toys in this stage of the baby's life – or with trying to teach your baby the alphabet or advanced arithmetic. During the first year, the motto is: keep it simple but safe.

Safety

Every developed country has one or more government agencies that keep an eye on product safety. You can rarely go wrong by following their recommendations, especially when it comes to toys. But given your child's vulnerability and the range of toys out there, it's good to be aware of some of the widespread pitfalls. Consider the following:

- Avoid products with ropes, cords, or cables exceeding about 10 inches. A child under 3 could accidentally strangle himself.
- Choose toys whose parts are too large to fit into your child's mouth (and therefore too large for him to swallow). Sharp edges and sharp-pointed protruding parts should be avoided.
- Choose glued wooden toys over materials that have been screwed together. Ask for wood that will not splinter, such as beechwood.
- Older articles intended for teething and biting, including plastic "teething rings" and all manner of pacifiers, may contain toxins. If

the product was manufactured prior to the year 2000, don't give it to your baby – not even if it was used without apparent negative consequences by an older child.

- Don't give toys whose contents may leak or spill due to biting or scratching.
- Frequently inspect the products in your baby's life. Discard broken toys.

Play and toys during the first year

This section lays out which games and toys are a good fit for each developmental phase.

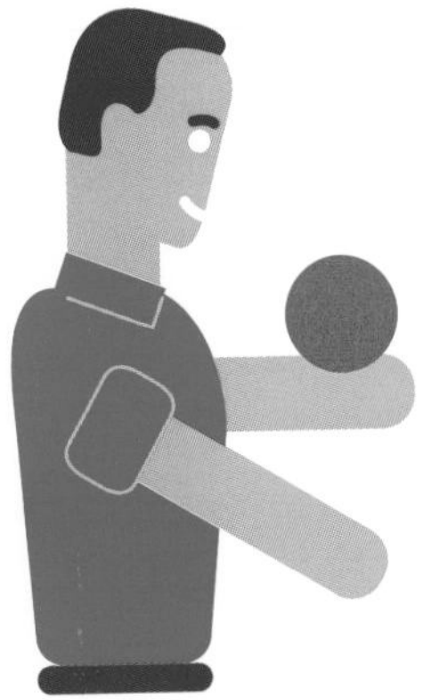

Zero to 3 months

After having gotten used to his strange new environment in the first few weeks after birth, your baby develops a growing curiosity for everything he sees and hears. You can indulge his natural inquisitiveness in many ways. Hold an object in front of his eyes and slowly move it from side to side. Hide your face behind a towel or a newspaper and watch his expression change as you re-emerge.

Mobile

The first thing that fascinates a baby in his new world is movement. Dynamic objects that form new patterns are a source of wonder. It's a good idea to hang a mobile over his crib or playpen.

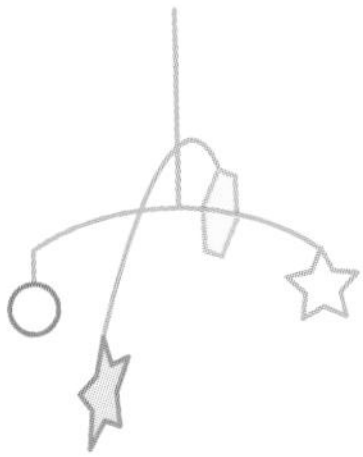

3 to 6 months

Put your baby on his back and let him kick his legs and flail his arms. In this phase, he'll begin discovering his hands and feet. Now that he recognizes your face, you'll probably feel tempted to display a range of facial expressions to keep him amused. Indulge him as much as you'd like.

Rattle

Since ancient times, rattles have been among the very first toys that babies got their hands on. The Romans gave their infants a *crepitaculum* (*crepare* means to produce sound). Rattles (made of earthenware, gold or silver) were long thought to drive away evil spirits, which is why babies would receive them after they'd been baptized. Rattles help develop a baby's grip, and their sound conveys the basic notion that actions lead to reactions. Splashing water during a bath drives home the very same principle.

Keychain

A modern variety of the old rattle. Don't let babies play with actual keys; we're talking about the large, colorful, plastic toys that rattle and jangle.

Play mat

Consists of colorful floor elements to which sound-producing elements have been affixed.

6 to 9 months

Once he's able to sit up, your child will literally have a firmer grasp of his environment. By picking up objects (and then tasting them!) he practices using his hands and fingers. Help him along by letting him play with soft, kneadable toys as well as objects like pan lids (if you can stand the racket). "Horsey" (bouncing him on your knee or your back) is another game he's now old enough to delight in. Increase the rhythm and accompany the ride with a simple story you make up. Looking at pictures together is also an activity he'll probably like by now.

Balls

Balloons or beach balls are great tools to get him into the soccer habit early.

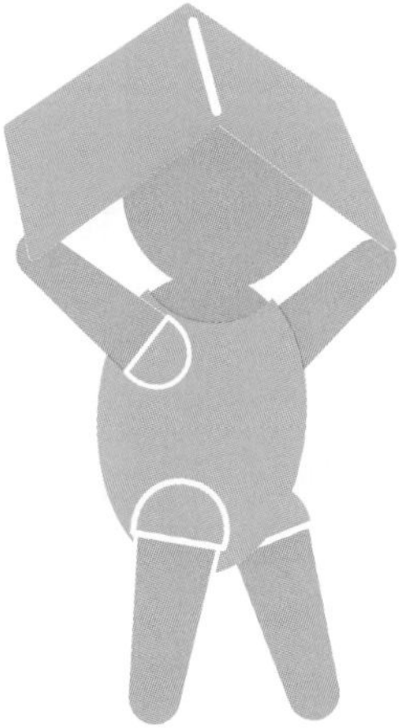

Books

Your baby is apt to like books with features that appeal to his still-developing vision and to his tactile pleasure. Preferably, choose large, simple images and thick pages of varying materials.

9 to 12 months

By now, your baby may crawl, so it's time to introduce him to hide and seek! Just letting him toss objects around (he'll be increasing his motor skills) will also hold considerable appeal for him. He will likely deepen his bond with you once he notices you retrieve whatever he throws, no matter where he throws it. Stimulate his fantasy by showing him that almost anything is a suitable object for play.

Sandbox

Your baby's still too young for sandcastles, but he probably does enjoy crawling through the sand and trying to grab it.

Walker

It'll be obvious when he's ready to learn to walk – don't push him too hard. But when the time comes, having a baby walker handy for him will boost his confidence as he takes his first steps.

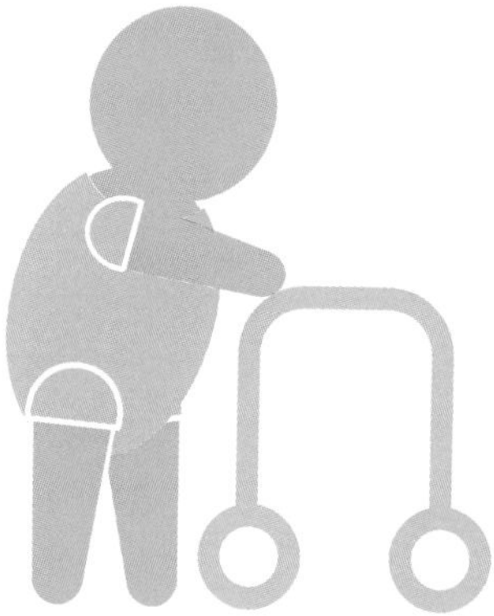

growth
& development

8

Pedigree and evolution of your product

Your product develops in an interactive process of aptitude and environment, biology and culture. Though this is true for all little humans, an individualized result is guaranteed – your product will be automatically outfitted with "unique selling points".

The tiniest person

The road from Adam's rib to the test tubes of 21st-century cloning labs is paved with theories about human development. One of the more colorful ones held that life forms start as tiny iterations of the eventual adult version. The most well-known proponent of this theory of preformationism might be famed natural scientist Antonie van Leeuwenhoek (1632–1723). Using a home-built microscope, he thought he saw an animalculus in a semen sample – a tiny person in a sperm cell, someone who would eventually spring from the womb jack-in-a-box-style. To this day, van Leeuwenhoek is widely recognized for his discovery of blood cells, sperm cells, and the microscope, but his observation of the animalculus is one of the dopiest bloopers in the annals of developmental science.

Natural selection

Van Leeuwenhoek was far from alone in espousing odd notions about life's genesis. Many great thinkers of their time contributed their own curious theories. Greek philosophers like Democritus and Anaximander almost stumbled upon the truth – or something close to it – with their musings that all creatures are born from mucky primordial slime that the sun somehow brought to life. On the other hand, Plato and Aristotle managed to freeze scientific progress with the theory that humankind is part of a closed system, a cosmic hierarchy in which every being has a fixed, unalterable place. And Christian thinkers further muddied the waters with their story of creation, in which God has absolute and universal power over both the birth of humankind and its demise (the apocalypse).

In 1859, a bombshell book blew many of these accepted beliefs to smithereens. In his breakthrough scientific book *The Origin of Species*, Charles Darwin unfolded his theories about the "tree of life". The British zoologist posited that all organisms on earth developed the way they did thanks to a protracted series of changes that take many generations to transfer completely. His theory of natural selection ("Survival of the fittest") created shockwaves: Darwin had the audacity to say that man was not made in God's image, but developed from his predecessors in the biological family tree: apes. After 150 years of denouncing Darwin for his heretical beliefs, the Vatican admitted a decade ago that the theory of evolution wasn't just quasi-scientific bilge – although the pontiff and his advisers still wanted God to receive His due: *"The human body may find its origin in pre-existing living matter, but the spiritual soul has been directly created by God,"* Pope John Paul wrote to the Papal Scientific Academy in 1996. But by then, the theory of evolution no longer needed encyclical approval. In the 1950s, Darwin's theory landed on solid ground with the discovery of DNA, life's building blocks. The resulting new science, genetics, provided the missing link for many remaining Darwin doubters. It became clear that DNA, present in every single cell of every organism, can endlessly replicate itself – and in the wake of that discovery, scientists learned how species continue to develop within evolution's framework. Your child is the product of the evolution of the species.

Mother Lucy

Your child's genetic code is structurally 98 per cent identical to that of a chimpanzee, and goes back along an evolutionary trail of some twenty million years. Chimps, gorillas, and bonobos (a smaller chimpanzee-like species) led to the birth of the human species. How and where the pedigrees crossed is still unclear. It's probable that our last shared ancestor, the *Orrorin tugenensis*, lived in the arid, relatively barren savannahs of East Africa. Two million years ago, a descendant of *tugenensis* produced offspring that began standing up straight and walking on two legs. While chimps and gorillas stayed behind both geographically and in terms of stilted evolution, their biped brethren started exploring. In 1974, a largely intact skeleton of such a hominid was found in Ethiopia, and the discoverers called it Lucy. Although Lucy and her friends were significant in the charted history of human development, her kind remained but a small dead branch of the hominid family tree.

In roughly the same time and location, a different hominid, *Homo habilis*, started a long and successful slog up the evolutionary path. Thanks to a bigger skull cavity and a varied high-protein diet that included meat and probably fish, his brain was able to develop fairly rapidly. *Homo habilis* began forming social networks, and became a primitive hunter who availed himself of simple tools. Beginning roughly 1.8 million years ago, *Homo erectus* then perfected these skills and expanded his species' habitat to Europe and Asia. About one- to two hundred thousand years ago, *Homo erectus* evolved into the grandparent of modern humans, *Homo sapiens*, whose lineage leads directly – via Neanderthal man, among others – to your child.

Gills

This evolutionary process repeats itself in your baby at dizzying speed. Just like more primitive organisms, your child begins life as a single cell, called a zygote. Within weeks he develops the tail of an amphibian and gills like those of a fish. Four months later we find his body covered in short, downy hairs called lanugo hair – an evolutionary residue that calls to mind the furry exterior of our ancient ancestors, a kind of pelt that he sheds only shortly before birth. The first days after the birth he possesses the instincts and reflexes of a small monkey clinging to its mother. A year later, he'll copy Lucy's long-ago example by standing upright.

The genesis of most of children's biological qualities is not yet entirely charted, but what is known is largely undisputed. The origins of his mental capacities, however, remain under discussion, as do the many theories about how he develops his cerebral skills and overall aptitudes.

According to the maturation theory, a baby is much like the small seed of a plant. All its qualities are solidly ensconced in the genetic material. You supply soil, water, and light, and the seed will sprout and grow. Behaviorism takes the opposite tack: that environment is everything. Originator John Watson, an American psychologist, once went as far as to say that he could mold a child into any kind of person: "Give me ten children and an environment in which to raise them. I guarantee that I can turn any child into whatever I want: a doctor, a lawyer, an artist, a business person, but also a beggar or a thief." The cognitive theory holds that there's an interaction between maturation and experience. Children have (or form) an image of how the world works, and subsequently examine if reality bears it out. Once the child has solved the conflict between reality and image, it is ready for the next step. Finally, according to Sigmund Freud's psychodynamic theory, the influence of experience triumphs over the power of the genes. The Austrian shrink believed that the child is the father of the man – in other words, whatever a child experiences in the first 5 years of his life will shape the rest of his development.

Of brains and bonds

Proponents of the cognitive theory have been getting more and more evidence-based support from brain researchers. The notion that the human mind develops according to a genetic blueprint has been discarded once and for all. At birth, a child's brain is still relatively barren, having gone through only 25 per cent of its growth. The organ contains about 100 billion neurons that are each capable of some 10,000 links to other cells. To build that kind of network, the brain needs lots of nutrients; it consumes 60 per cent of the infant's energy supply. The links between the neurons are mostly formed as a result of the baby's sensory experiences. Through environmental stimuli, including touch, movement, and language, networks are created that implement conceptual structure and the opportunity for further expansion. In the first 3 years of the baby's life, brain structure grows to 85 per cent. Experiences in the earliest stages of an infant's life help shape the brain. Positive experiences provide enrichment; neglect, violence, and abuse, however, can stunt normal growth. Not only the quality and intensity of such experiences is important; *when* they take place can carry equal weight. The brain develops in a number of phases. One critical period occurs when neurons initiate and finalize their connections to handle complex tasks such as focusing the eyes and depth perception. When the child undergoes negative experiences at this stage, the quality of the created function can be affected.

Patterns of bonding

It is up to you to ensure that your child gets plentiful positive experiences during the crucial first years. As one of the child's primary caregivers, you help supply the foundation for his emotional, social, and intellectual development. This process is called bonding. The first year of the baby's life is the most sensitive period for creating this bond, especially the second half of the year, when your baby begins to form a picture of the people taking care of him. At the same time, he'll be busy creating an awareness and image of himself, based on the responses and stimuli he receives from his environment. Through the interaction between the self-image and the picture he has of his caregivers, he weaves a subconscious bond. Behavioral patterns and the nature and intensity of the emotions in a relationship find a permanent place in this structure, and are likely to exert a strong influence on the relationships that the child will form with others later in life. Social scientists discern several different patterns of bonding – most prominently, the "securely bonded" and the "insufficiently bonded" child. The former reacts positively to the return of the mother or the father, and is open to (or keen on) being comforted. The insufficiently bonded child may ignore the returning parent and has the tendency to explore his environment in a hyperactive manner.

Motherly love

John Bowlby is a pioneer in the field of research that studies the child-parent relationship. The British psychiatrist became fascinated by the topic when, in an institution for "difficult" children, he observed a withdrawn teenager who'd never known a stable mother figure. Bowlby decided to study child psychiatry and psychoanalysis to sharpen his thoughts about the influence of the family on the development of sons and daughters. After a series of observations of motherless children, he published the first part of his famous *Attachment Theory* in 1957. In that study, he sought to demonstrate that the bonding between mother and child is of great significance for the success of relationships the child will form later in life. Bowlby defined bonding behavior as a genetically programmed behavioral pattern that the child displays to guarantee the physical proximity of the primary caregiver. If the child's needs remain unmet, his reactions include protest, desperation, withdrawal (un-bonding), and denial – in that order. The high (even mythical) value that Bowlby and others assign to motherhood doesn't quite gel with today's practices and theories; and the "rose-tinted" ideal which magazines, books, and advertisers still trot out to hold women hostage to an exclusive mother role evaporates when the facts are scrutinized. Multiple historical studies have made clear that our ideas about the importance of parental love have varied greatly through the ages, influenced by a given society's economic, political, and cultural characteristics. For instance, the relatively passive involvement of modern western dads is a marked contrast to the fathers among the Aka pygmies, a tribe of hunter-gatherers that lives in the jungles of the Congo. Because all members of the tribe are needed for the hunt, the strongest shoulders carry the heaviest burden: the fathers tote the babies day after day in a body carrier, and only break contact when it's time for the mothers to breastfeed the children. If the mother is absent and the child is hungry, an Aka man will offer the baby one of his own nipples, to calm it. Active, involved western moms might also be amazed by how much mother roles have changed in their own part of the world. In the Middle Ages, mothers of some means would habitually part with their babies and give them to a rural wet nurse for 3 to 4 years. Only when the child was already an accomplished talker would he be welcomed back into the family, but the mother's involvement usually remained limited; educating the offspring, for instance, was widely seen as the father's exclusive turf.

Artificial mothers

In addition to various cultural-historic comparative studies, the mother myth is also undermined by psychological research. The assumption that motherly love is an exclusive byproduct of breastfeeding a child, for instance, turns out to be wholly erroneous. In 1957, the same year in which Bowlby published his *Attachment Theory*, the American psychologist Harry Harlow devised a range of experiments into the origin of love. Harlow was skeptical that the bond between a mother and her child had much to do with the food she proffered. To prove his point, he worked with a group of macaques, long-tailed monkeys who respond to sensory stimuli much in the way that human babies do. Shortly after the birth of a number of baby macaques, Harlow isolated them from their mothers. The young animals were then kept in a space with two "artificial mothers"; one metal wireframe model and one made from soft cotton, heated by a lamp. Only the metal mother was outfitted with a "nipple", a rubber teat attached to a milk bottle. The baby monkeys only sought her company when they were hungry. As soon as they were sated, they nestled against the cotton mother. And as soon as the cotton mother was equipped with a milk-dispensing teat, the macaques lost all interest in the wireframe mother. Harlow tested this intriguing result in another study. He again isolated newborn macaques from their biological mothers, then divided the group of infants in two. Each group had access to only one of the artificial mothers, but this time both mothers had a feeding teat. Both groups consumed the same amount of food, and there was no discernible difference in how members of each group developed in size and weight. Biologically, the metal mother's "children" developed as well as the young macaques fed by the cotton mother, but psychologically the differences were not subtle. The former group exhibited fear and frustration, and its members proved unable to have sexual dalliances with macaques who were in the cotton mother's group. Even Harlow himself was surprised by the outcome. "We'd assumed that physical touching would be an important part of bonding – but that the importance of food would be so clearly overshadowed was an eye-opener," he noted. "It's now an established fact that working women do not have to rush home just on account of their biological qualities as mothers. We need to realize that men, too, have the essential qualities needed to raise children."

Blood bond

Other studies into the parent-child bond have brought to light the fact that a blood bond (biological connection) between parent and child isn't a necessity, as the child will generally bond just as well with a non-biological parent. The gender of the parent or caregiver is of no importance to the successful forging of a bond. The quality of the relationship is more important than the quantity: in other words, the degree to which the parent/caregiver meets the needs of the child matters more than the number of hours he or she puts in. Parent and child have to literally form an understanding to make for a safe and successful bonding experience. During the child's first 3 years, he will grow from being completely dependent to being focused on exploration and becoming his own person. This evolution, which is necessary for the child's emotional balance, is only possible when he finds physical and emotional security by bonding with an adult, or adults, who become focal points of his little world. From this safe haven, which is the child's base, he will go out and explore.

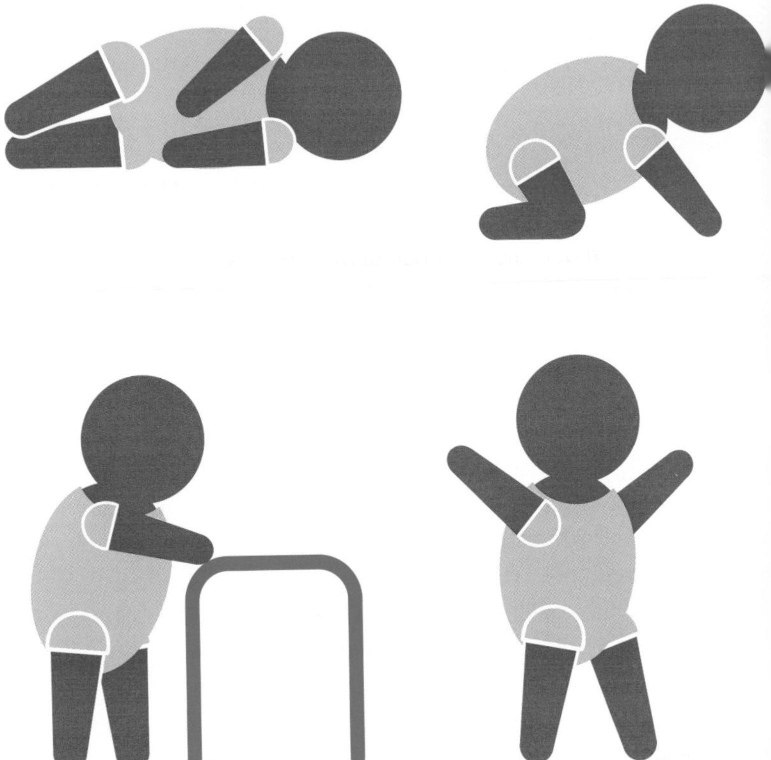

Development of motor skills

Not so very long ago, scientists regarded a baby as a creature that was essentially deaf, mute, and blind. Now, infants get a lot more recognition, as they're often seen as sophisticated little learning machines that acquire some pretty advanced skills through trial and error. The development of motor skills typically takes place in a set, seemingly preprogrammed order: from the baby's head to his toes, and from his rump spreading outwards. Your baby first gains control of the muscles closest to the brain. For example, before he can begin to learn to crawl, he has to find a way to keep his head balanced. Muscle control goes from rough to fine, resulting in ever-more delicate, purposeful movements. Cultural customs can influence the development of motor skills. Children who are frequently carried on a parent's back in a sling or another baby carrier tend to learn to walk sooner, often when they're as young as 10 months old. The position in the sling or carrier forces them to gain control of the muscles in the neck and midriff, a feat which in turn promotes a solid sense of physical balance.

In its first year, a child goes through roughly 5 stages of mental and motor-skill development.

Month 0: a sleepy-head with reflexes

- Is asleep a lot of the time. Recognizes the basic patterns of a human face, especially the eyes.
- Recognizes the mother's voice, distinguishing it from strangers' voices.
- Responds to every face with social behavior such as babbling or crying. This is essentially survival behavior, designed to keep the caregiver close by.

- Has the following reflexes:
  - **Sucking reflex** Activated by brushing a nipple (or a substitute) against the baby's cheek.
  - **Moro or "startle" reflex** Triggered by unexpected sounds or movements. The baby stretches his limbs as if asking for an embrace.
  - **Palmar grasp reflex** Newborns curl their fingers and toes when they feel a touch on their palms or soles. Eventually, this develops into a full-fledged grip.
  - **Stepping reflex** When the child is held up (supported underneath his arms), he'll make walking motions.
  - **Balance reflex** When the baby's face is turned to one side, he'll often stretch out the arm on the opposite side by way of correction.
  - **Defensive reflex** When an object approaches the baby's face, he'll turn to the side in a maneuver of deflection or avoidance.
  - **Dive reflex** Activated when the baby goes underwater. Metabolism and heart rate go down, the windpipe is shut off, and oxygen-rich blood is pumped to the heart and brain to increase chances of survival. There are indications that the child uses the same reflex during birth. With infant swim lessons, this instinct can be shaped into a deliberate, acquired ability to float, swim, and submerge.

Most of these reflexes fade and disappear after 3 to 6 months, as soon as the baby is able to more or less master his movements.

Months 0–3: the observer

- Produces sounds that resemble rudimentary language.
- Begins to show an interest in more complex visual patterns.

- Sees a moving and immovable object as two different things.
- Turns head and/or eyes in the direction of a sound source.
- Recognizes the pattern in a human face. Actions beget reactions.
- Produces a social smile in response to faces and high-pitched voices.
- Is able to distinguish the mother's face from that of a stranger.
- Grabs (clumsily) at objects.
- Gains more control over head and neck muscles.
- Sensitive to the presence of other babies (resulting in looking/staring).

Months 3–6: the grabber

- Takes in objects' abstract characteristics. Distinguishes between round objects and ones with corners.
- Distinguishes between methods of expression (anger, affection).
- Can express sadness, anger, and anxiety himself.
- Returns smiles in kind.
- Develops a personal temperament.
- Speaks a more or less universal baby language.

- Develops an interest in objects and seeks out new ones when the old ones become familiar. Distinguishes people from objects. Focuses on a few people. Develops clear preferences.
- Handles objects with more sophistication, and, when grabbing for them, takes into account the speeds at which these things may move. Adjusts the shape of his hand to the object he's about to grab.
- Corrects his balance.
- Can lift his head and upper torso a bit, and discovers he can move about a little while lying on his stomach.
- Increased sensitivity to the presence of other babies; wants to touch them.

Months 6–9: the crawler

- Distinguishes between male and female voices. Can tell emotions apart when expressed by those voices.
- Moves from baby language to the sounds of his mother tongue.
- Begins to see commonality in patterns. Can tell men and women apart by their gender-specific facial features.

- His first tooth comes in!
- Bonds to a parent/caregiver and to several other persons with whom he feels safe. Feels and expresses anxiety when left alone.
- Is able to get up on hands and knees and to stay upright.
- Turns from lying on his stomach to lying on his back, and vice versa. Starts to crawl.
- Exchanges smiles with other babies.

Months 9–12: the little wanderer

- Has a will of his own.
- Searches and finds attractive objects.
- Starts to imitate sounds and words.
- Can crawl, and can walk with a little help.
- Further develops reaching and grabbing.
- Can adjust his motions to the object he's focusing on, such as a rolling ball.
- Plays simple games with other babies.
- Develops rudimentary self-awareness.

Weight and length

Monitoring your baby's health and progress comes down in large part to measuring three things: weight, length, and head circumference. Weight and length may provide indications of possible growth impediments; the head circumference is a measure of how the baby's brain is developing. At birth, all the baby's vital organs are complete (if small), but the brain is the obvious exception here. A brain that grows too fast can be a sign of hydrocephalus, a condition in which a child has an excess of brain fluid that puts pressure on (and stretches) the fontanelles. A brain that grows too slowly, on the other hand, can indicate nutritional defects. The results of the three measurements are expressed in so-called percentiles, a statistical number that tells you how your child is doing compared to others of the same age. If your child scores 75 on, say, the weight curve, this means that 75 per cent of children of the same age weigh less, and 25 per cent weigh more.

Determining your product's weight

First, step on the scale yourself, and note your weight. Then take the (naked) baby in your arms and step back onto the scale. Subtract your weight from the total to arrive at the baby's weight. Use the graph on the following page to see where your baby ranks and how he's progressing.

Determining your product's length

Put your baby on his back on a large sheet of paper. With a pen or pencil, mark the paper just above the top of his head. Then extend his legs and make a similar mark right below his heel. Use the graph on the following page to see where your baby ranks and how he's progressing.

Product weight

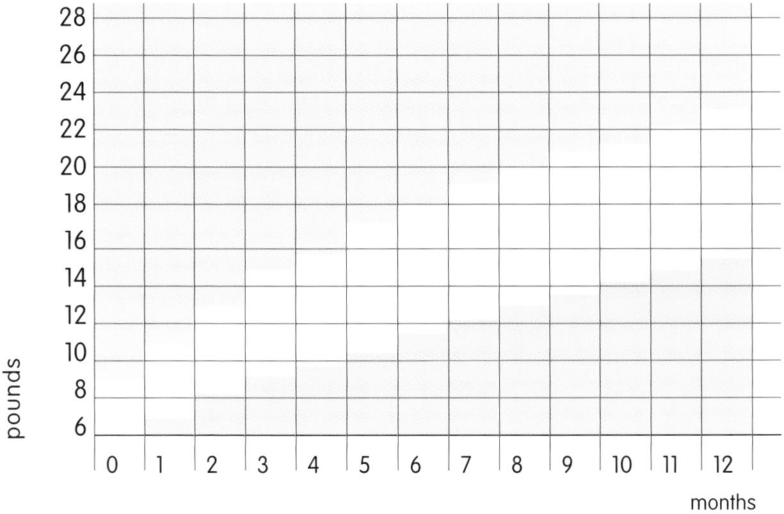

Product length

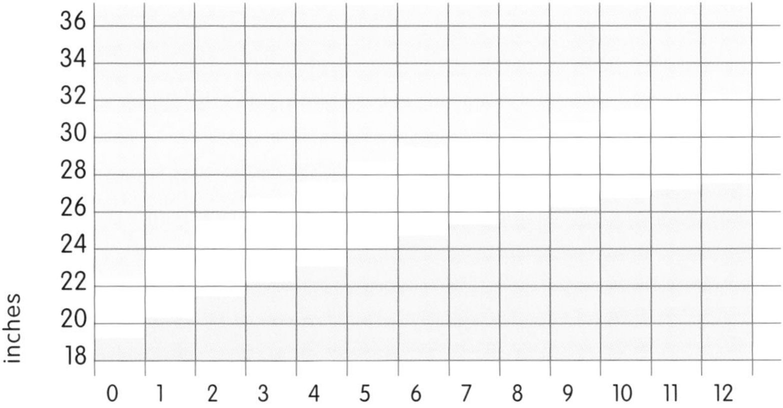

! Most children follow the growth curve they start at birth. Minor deviations upwards or downwards are normal, and each child grows at his own speed. However, if there are dramatic peaks and valleys in your child's curve, see a physician.

Temperament

Temperament is a catch-all term for an individual's behavioral tendencies and reaction patterns. During the first months of a baby's life, not much can be said with certainty about his character; his behavior is still influenced to a great extent by temporary factors such as the recovery from the birth process, hormones, and food. Around the 4th month, these factors begin to fade in importance, and make way for a clearer view of your child's personality. Psychologists use the following terms to get a grip on a child's temperament.

- **Activity level** – Is your child very active or exceedingly calm?
- **Regularity/routine** – How predictable are his eating and sleeping patterns?
- **Approach** – How does he react to unfamiliar people and new situations?
- **Adaptability** – How does your child handle changes to his schedule or an interruption of his activities?
- **Sensitivity** – How does he react to harsh light and loud sounds?
- **Mood** – Does he appear happy most of the time?
- **Intensity** – How adamant is he in letting you know precisely how he feels?
- **Focus** – Can your child play with one toy for an extended period, or does he choose different toys in rapid succession?

Psychologists don't always agree with each other about the true dimensions of the human temperament. However, there is a consensus that behavioral patterns are largely present from birth, and that these patterns are reinforced or suppressed by a person's interactions with his environment, and in particular with parents and siblings.

9

Consultants

Consultants

Meet your advisers

As a baby manager, you'll meet both "internal" and "external" consultants. You hire external ones for a specific duration; internal advisers will be guiding you through the entire product development. The advice of neither category should be taken lightly; then again, no matter how much experience and expertise they claim, you must ultimately find your own path.

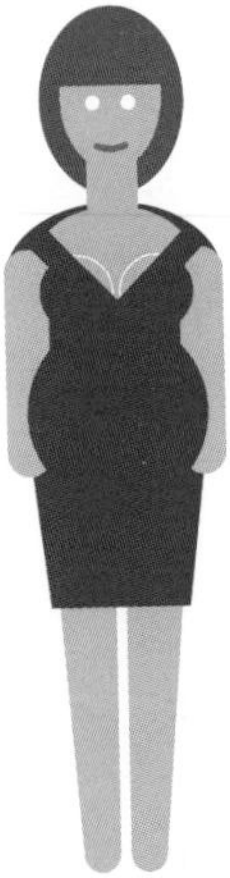

Internal consultant: producer

Description: Young(ish) lady responsible for the assembly process you set in motion.

Call in: Doesn't need to be called in. She will dispense her advice whether or not you ask her.

Method: Her suggestions seek to increase your involvement during the product development process. Likely recommendations include:

- Get rid of the convertible and buy a safe, roomy, sensible car.
- Improve your financial security.
- Consider buying roomier living quarters. Yeah, that means the suburbs.
- Stop smoking and cut down on beer and booze.
- Love me!

During the assembly, she aims primarily for emotional security; after delivery, financial security begins to loom large.

Duration: Unlimited.

User tip: Let her know how much you appreciate her advice; maintaining her emotional balance is paramount.

Cost: Priceless.

External consultant: certified nurse or midwife

Description: A nurse with a special training in low-risk pregnancies and childbirth. Her work consists of providing information, involving you and your partner in decision-making, making a birth plan, and providing care before, during, and after the baby is born. She – a *he* is a rare phenomenon – works in a hospital, a birthing center, in partnership with a doctor or from her home. In most European countries, the midwife is the primary caregiver during pregnancy and birth. In the U.S., midwives attend about 8 per cent of births, a number that has been increasing steadily. When a woman requires care beyond her area of expertise, a midwife will call in an obstetrician. The two professionals are supposed to complement each other, but conflicts ignite easily as obstetricians generally prefer a more active approach, while midwives are taught not to intervene unless necessary. A midwife generally encourages natural childbirth: she relies less on pain relief, such as epidurals, and uses fewer interventions than obstetricians do. But this also means that if a midwife misinterprets a situation during a home birth, you might have to race to the hospital with your dilating wife in the back seat. An unlikely but hardly uncommon event, especially in the Netherlands where more than thirty per cent of all births take place at home. After giving birth to our first child, my wife shared a hospital room with a woman who had been hoisted out of her 5th-floor Amsterdam apartment by a fire-brigade crane. At 7 centimeters dilated she had found herself unable to use the stairs.

Call in: Your producer will want to find a midwife a couple of months after assembly has begun. The midwife will likely insist on personal checkups starting in the 12th week. A month before the scheduled delivery, these checkups will occur weekly.

Method: In the old days, the midwife performed a particularly intimate task. She massaged the inner vaginal parts of the laboring woman with a special oil made from young mackerel, musk, ambergris, civet and other ingredients, as prescribed in a medieval recipe. The midwife carried on until the woman reached an orgasm. The climax was considered necessary to relieve tension. Today, the midwife's job is still intimate but surely less arousing. During a checkup, she will generally perform these tasks:

- Measure blood pressure and weight
- Check iron level in the blood (anemia detection)
- Gentle pushing and prodding of the abdomen to determine if the product is growing well and in the right position
- Listen to the producer's heartbeat
- Inquire after producer's physical and mental state
- Inquire after the producer's diet
- Have a conversation about future checkups and procedures, and about the intended delivery address.

Duration: A checkup takes about 40 minutes.

User tip: Your producer will appreciate your involvement and company during the checkups. Soothe possible anxieties and accompany her during the checkups.

Cost: Count on approximately $3,000. This includes prenatal tests, exams in the clinic, the home birth itself, and exams post-delivery and six weeks thereafter. Check carefully whether your insurance covers the services of a midwife. While you're at it, check whether she is certified according to state law.

External consultant: Obstetrician

Description: Doctor with special training in prenatal care, labor, birth, high-risk pregnancies, and surgery.

Call in: If you choose a midwife, you might not see this specialist at all. But you can also leave everything to an obstetrician.

Method: Throughout the pregnancy, the obstetrician monitors the gestational progress. During labor and birth, he – males still slightly outnumber females in this profession – is more likely to resort to drugs, technology, and surgery than a family doctor or midwife would. Obstetricians are said to have become more responsive to nontraditional preferences couples might have, such as the help of doulas and softening up the clinical hospital atmosphere with music and mood lighting.

Duration: Depends.

User tip: Especially if things go wrong, it helps to have familiarized yourself with some obstetrician's lingo. While she's expecting, expect the unexpected: you could end up in a stressful situation where your exhausted and drugged wife is unable to make decisions or to speak at all, while the obstetrician is contemplating delivery by vacuum extraction or forceps. At least, I was glad I didn't need subtitles when I watched all these white coats discussing delivery options around my wife's bed.

Cost: $2,500 to $7,500 for general prenatal care and a delivery without medical complications. Check your insurance to see what's covered.

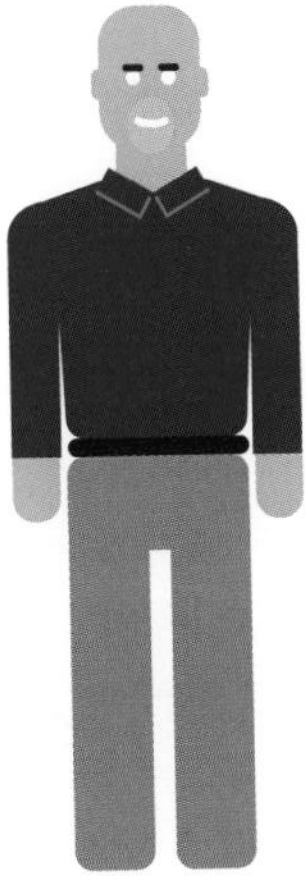

Internal consultant: your dad
Description: Middle-aged or older, in large part responsible for the product that is you.
Call in: No call necessary. He'll be there.
Method: Depending on his character and your relationship, he will either want to be involved or remain at a distance. After being apprised of the fact that the assembly has been irrevocably set in motion, he'll be looking for a moment to have a good father-son talk. Some of his tips have withstood the test of the ages; others, however, are way past the sell-by date.
Duration: Unlimited.
User tip: The period from assembly to delivery offers a string of opportunities to strengthen your bond. Enjoy reminiscing together: after the delivery, your life might be too hectic for such luxuries.
Cost: Priceless.

Internal consultant: your mom
Description: Middle-aged or older, in large part responsible for the product that is you. Sound familiar?
Call in: See under "your dad".
Method: No matter your relationship, she'll be dispensing advice. And dispensing it. And dispensing some more.
Duration: Unlimited.
User tip: Her practical advice on baby care is worth listening to. Really. Let her regale you with stories about her own assemblies and deliveries, but ensure

she doesn't overload your producer with a profusion of well-intended tips.
Cost: Priceless.

External consultant: maternity nurse

Description: Skilled health care professional who provides an array of care during but mostly in the days after delivery. Common in most European countries, Australia and New Zealand. Rare in the U.S.
Call in: Depends on your preference (and on your insurance). You can choose to rely on family or friends to help you out in the first days after birth, or you can book a maternity nurse. Do so well in advance.
Method: Helps in establishing a routine for feeding, dressing, and bathing the baby. Deals with the laundry, sterilizing bottles, and preparing meals. Gives first-time mothers advice on breastfeeding and any problems arising from it. Her primary interest is the well-being of the mother and the newborn. Don't expect her to look after any other siblings – or after you, the dad.
Duration: Depends on your preference. She can come for a day or two, or for a whole week. If your product was delivered by caesarean and you don't have any other help, you'll want her to stay longer.
User tip: Watch carefully how she handles your kid because here's a real Baby Manager at work. Where you might think your product is as vulnerable as a piece of rice paper, notice how she firmly grips the baby, picking him up or toweling his back. Don't sulk if

she's ignoring you, she won't stay forever. Make the best of it and enjoy these wonderful first few days at home.
Cost: Count on a minimum $125 a day. Your insurance might cover the costs.

Internal consultant: your mother-in-law
Description: Producer of your producer.
Call in: See under "your dad".
Method: She will lavish attention on your producer. If they enjoy a good relationship, tips, suggestions, and stories from the old days will pour forth from her always-busy mouth.
Duration: Unlimited.
User tip: Treasure her babysitting capacity. Work on maintaining a good relationship, though it's OK to draw a line in the sand if she goes from helpful to meddlesome.
Cost: Priceless.

Internal consultant: your father-in-law
Description: Manager of your producer.
Call in: See under "your dad".
Method: If he was slightly cool to you before, he'll probably buddy up, seeing as you and the producer are now past the point of no return. His advice is intended to guarantee an auspicious start for the spin-off of his product. He'll emphasize themes like financial security, suitable housing, insurance, and may discuss the finer points of inheritance law.
Duration: Unlimited.

User tip: Your father-in-law can be an ally. Get on his good side. Remember: this is a point of no return for you, too. Just don't let him dictate your decisions.
Cost: Priceless.

External consultant: your baby's healthcare provider

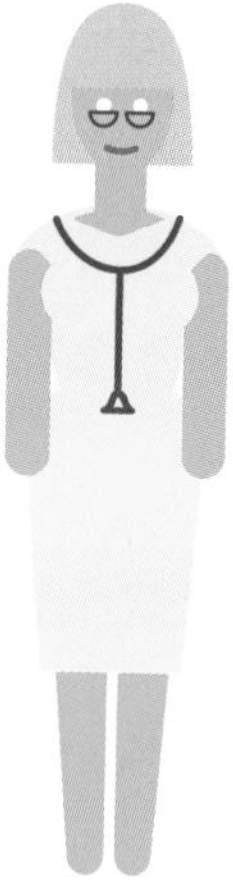

Description: Could be your family physician or a pediatrician.
Call in: In some countries you'll automatically receive a phone call from a nurse wishing to set up an appointment. Elsewhere, you'll have to arrange a checkup yourself.
Method: During the checkups, the doctor will meticulously monitor motor skills, sensory development, weight, length, and the (emotional) maturation of your product. He'll collect all his data according to a standardized method that allows for comparisons between individual results and baby benchmarks. Timely detection of possible deviations is what this is all about, so that specialist treatment can be called in if necessary. Abnormalities are found in 2 to 3 per cent of all babies. In two-thirds of these cases, the defect consists of a lag in developmental or linguistic skills. Hearing tests and vaccinations are also part of these so-called "well-baby visits".
Duration: A checkup takes about 20 to 30 minutes. The primary well-baby visit usually takes place within a few weeks of the delivery, continuing at intervals of 2 months during the first half a year, and at 3-month intervals until he's 2 years old.
User tip: Don't let your wife do the honors all the time. Enjoy the

surprised look of all the ladies in the waiting room if you show up. Go at least once and do your fatherly duty: bring your camera and record how the nurse tries to persuade your kid to lie flat enough to be measured, or to sit still on a scale long enough to get weighed. And don't forget to ask all the questions you want, including on topics like sex and birth control.

Safety procedures

No, you're not done yet. To ensure a rewarding life cycle for your product, safety is key in the first few days and weeks. So here's some background on safety procedures you will run into.

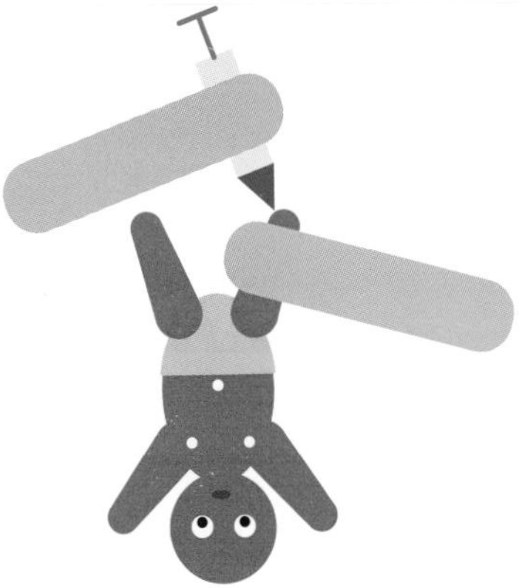

Heel prick

Within the first week of delivery, and often within 48 hours, a sample of your product's blood will be obtained through a heel prick. In the lab, the blood is then analyzed for rare but serious diseases such as hypothyroidism (underactivity of the thyroid gland), PKU (phenylketonuria, a disorder brought on by deficiency of an enzyme necessary for brain development), galactosemia (affects the ability to properly metabolize the sugar galactose), and sickle-cell disease (a disorder of the blood caused by an inherited abnormal hemoglobin). In the western world, almost all children are tested for these disorders. These genetic diseases are currently incurable, but early treatment can prevent irreversible damage.

Hearing screening

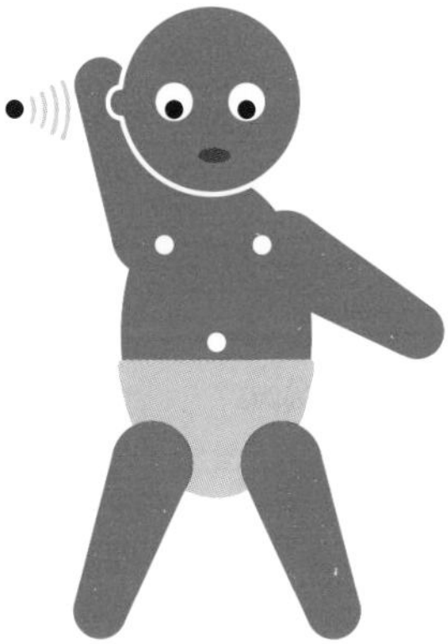

Hearing is an essential feature of your product. If yours isn't equipped with a system that hears sounds in all pitches, it will experience difficulty in learning to talk. Serious deafness is something you will notice yourself, but a diminished acuteness of hearing will most likely escape non-experts. Therefore, almost all western countries have implemented screening protocols to test your product's audio capabilities. These screenings sometimes even occur prior to mother and child leaving the hospital or birthing clinic. Until a couple of years ago, the baby was brought into a room where real sounds were generated, by instruments, speech or handclapping, while the nurse would observe the baby's response. Nowadays, this classic Ewing Distraction Test is usually replaced by a high-tech approach. Two different methods are used: the Auditory Brainstem Response test (ABR) and the Otoacoustic Emission (OAE) screening. During the ABR test, electrodes are attached to your baby's head to record electrical activity from the auditory nerve (the hearing nerve) and other parts of the brain. OAE screening involves an intricate device that could have been imagined by Q, James Bond's gadget man. The device, a small probe containing a minuscule microphone and speaker, is inserted into your baby's ear, usually while he sleeps. The probe generates sounds and records an echo that rolls back from the cochlea. This echo, called the Kemp echo after British researcher David Kemp who discovered the phenomenon in 1979, is the actual otoacoustic emission, a sound reflected by the ear itself in response to an external sound. During the test, the emissions are presented on a computer screen. Either an audiologist, or a healthcare provider with some audiological training, analyzes which external sounds yield a response. If the inner ear reacts to sounds that are crucial for speech comprehension, your product receives a stamp of approval.

Vaccination

To protect your product against contagious diseases that used to claim many lives, you should see to it that your baby receives proper vaccinations. Vaccination isn't mandatory, but most parents go for the shots, albeit not always according to the schedules that are recommended by health authorities. In the U.S. for instance, only about 70 per cent of babies and young children have been adequately immunized. Pay attention to the time frame: many children get their shots too early or too close together, in which case the vaccines aren't as effective as they should be. Guidelines vary by country.

Objections?

A small but steadily increasing number of parents refuse to have their kids vaccinated. They may feel that way for religious reasons or, strange as it may seem, for health reasons. The vaccination opponents claim that our immune system is strong enough to fight intruding viruses and would only be weakened by vaccines. You can find (many) more arguments on sites like www.vaccineriskawareness.com.

Needless to say, official health organizations worldwide agree on the need for vaccinations. If you choose not to vaccinate your child, keep two things in mind. Foreign travel might become difficult or impossible as many countries require proof of vaccination. And almost all schools, before admitting your child, want to see evidence that he is up to date on all his shots.

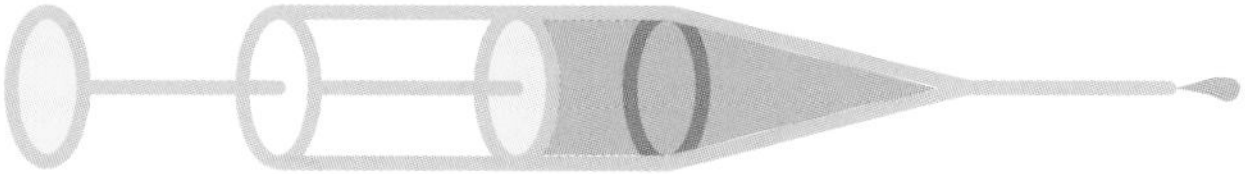

10 Automation

From Teddycam to GPS tracking

From footie pajamas with movement-detecting sensors to implantable chips that let you monitor the exact whereabouts of your product: baby managers can't escape automation.

Communication tools

The classical baby monitor that had to be wired from the living room to the nursery is pretty much a thing of the past. Modern baby monitoring devices are portable and work wirelessly (with radio waves), over your home's electrical grid, or through the phone lines.

Cordless baby monitor

Technology: Sends and receives radio waves. Newer-generation devices are less susceptible to interference and noise than earlier models.

Options:

- Permanently on, or sound-activated
- Out-of-range warning
- Identification feature: when the sound from the transmitter kicks in, you'll also hear a user-selectable digital beep telling you that's really your baby stirring, and not the neighbors' rugrat.
- Volume control
- Two-way feature, allows you to talk back
- Built-in digital lullabies
- Temperature indicator
- User-selectable channels
- DECT: Digital Enhanced Cordless Communications Technology that fully digitizes transmission, keeps interference at bay, and is virtually impervious to eavesdroppers.

Range: about 300–1,200 feet

Pros:

- Allows relatively unrestricted mobility of the receiver
- Many choices
- Affordable

Cons:

- May be prone to interference if the frequencies are in use by amateur radio stations, CB enthusiasts, or other people with baby monitors; but if you set the transmitter to "continuous", you can often push out the interfering source.
- Without DECT (see above), risk of eavesdroppers.

Electrical-system baby monitor

Technology: Plug and play. Just plug the transmitter into a wall outlet in the baby's room, and power the receiver through an outlet in your own space. The sound is transmitted through the electrical wires in your walls.

Range: 30–100 feet

Pros:

- Simplicity

Cons:

- Other equipment, such as TVs and computers, sometimes interpret the sound signal as a sign of power loss or a brownout, which could hamper those devices' peak performance and reliability.

Baby monitor with camera

Technology: You can choose between a surveillance camera that plugs into your TV or video-recording device, and a pricier alternative that's tailored to baby watching. The latter technology usually consists of a receiver (with an LCD screen) that communicates wirelessly with the nursery-cam. Some cameras are hidden in a teddy bear or another toy.

Options:

- Integrated infrared light can make your child visible in the dark without disturbing his sleep
- Choose between sound or images, or select both
- Sound activation – the camera turns on automatically when the baby produces sound

Range: 30–40 feet

Pros:

- Complete control and peace of mind
- Observe your child during the night
- Suitable for different applications

Cons:

- Pricey

Baby monitor combined with cell phone

Technology: It's a hi-tech baby monitor with a twist – it knows to reach you on your cell phone anywhere you go. The device can be plugged into any standard telephone wall outlet. Once the transmitter detects a sound (you can set the sensitivity of the microphone), it dials a number you've pre-programmed, such as that of your cell phone. If you have caller ID on your phone, you'll be able to tell it's the monitor calling you. You can also do the reverse: call the monitor and listen in. Extra inputs are suitable for connecting a motion sensor or a fire alarm.

Range: unlimited

Pros:

- Works even when you're abroad
- Monitor your child anytime, anywhere
- No interference

Cons:

- Needs to be programmed
- Cost of calls could be substantial

Two-way radio with baby monitor function

Technology: Two-way radios, a.k.a. walkie-talkies, tend to be fairly powerful transmitters/receivers with a corresponding range and good sound quality. Baby-monitoring walkie-talkies are often equipped with a VOX (speech-activated) feature.

Range: up to 0.7 miles.

Pros:

- Not susceptible to poor reception caused by concrete structures
- Multiple applications
- Radio quality

Cons:

- Needs to be programmed
- Some basic knowledge of radio technology required

Protection against SIDS (Sudden Infant Death Syndrome)

The risk of SIDS (also known as "crib death") can be lessened with some of these electronic tools:

Baby monitor with motion sensor

Technology: The basic version of this device consists of two mats with motion sensors and a separate "guard unit". The mats go in the baby's crib, underneath his mattress, where the sensors record every tiny movement, even the rising and falling of the baby's chest during normal breathing. An alarm goes off if the sensors detect no motion for more than 20 seconds. An expanded version is available for parents who'd like a wireless, rechargeable, portable receiver.

Range: 30–40 feet

Pros:

- Peace of mind

Cons:

- Causes needless panic in case of false alarms.

SIDS monitor

Technology: This system, trademarked as Mamagoose, consists of pajamas with built-in biological sensors whose task is to record the baby's heart rate and breathing. A separate unit placed next to the crib receives these data, and compares them to the benchmarks for healthy babies. If the system detects a problem, it notifies you with an alarm. The vital signs recorded by the machine can be analyzed by a doctor. The father of the Mamagoose is Stefaan Devolder, an engineer whose sister and daughter both died of SIDS.

The SIDS monitor was developed by the Belgian firm Verhaert, a hi-tech company that specializes in bringing spacecraft technology to everyday products. The European space organization ESA and the Belgian government helped with the financing. The biomedical lab of the University of Brussels participated in the research.

Sleepy time

Womb-simulating teddy bear

Technology: "Slumber bear" with sound and motion sensors. The bear's belly simulates "sounds from the womb" when the baby moves, cries, or shakes the toy. Developed by a physician. The removable speaker can be affixed to the crib.

Intelligent night light

Technology: Night light with sound sensor. When the baby starts crying, the light turns itself up automatically and the device plays a simple, soothing tune. You can also record your own voice onto the device. The duration of the lighting period is user-settable. The lullaby sound cuts off after four minutes.

Magic theater

Technology: Baby-friendly slide projector is styled like a playful pig's snout. Projects visual patterns on the wall or the ceiling while playing soft music. The device comes with different slides corresponding to the baby's developmental phase – or design your own.

Digital Trackers

Observing your baby in the nursery is perhaps only the beginning. Soon, keeping tabs on junior will be a worldwide game.

Implantable chip

Technology: As revolutionary as it is controversial. Brought to market by U.S. company Applied Digital, this invention means peace of mind for some parents – and represents a chilling Orwellian future to others. The trackable chip, roughly the size of a grain of rice, can be implanted behind a young child's collarbone. It can transmit and receive, and contains both GPS technology and a bio-monitoring system. The so-called "digital angel" puts fears about lost and kidnapped children to rest; you'll always know where your child is, and where he has been. The chip had been in use only in lab animals and livestock until Applied Digital, in 2004, received permission from the U.S. government to begin human implantation.

Lots of people feel uncomfortable about the technology, including one theologian who roared that he saw the chip as the biblical "sign of the beast" that heralded the end of times. In an effort to assuage some of the concerns, Applied Digital then launched a line of digital trackers that are considered less intrusive, like the "Hugs" and "Halo" models. These "infant protection systems" offer features similar to those in the Digital Angel chip, but the chip is embedded in a bracelet, not under the skin.

Kiddie mobile

Technology: Not some mobile art for hanging over your offspring's crib, but kid-friendly cell phones/GPS trackers that could make your child the envy of less digitally advantaged tykes. There has been

persistent anxiety about the possible damage that cell phone radiation can inflict on the brain – concerns that are magnified when the cell phone users are young children. Government health advisories have stated that there's no reason to restrict the use of cellular devices to anyone over 2 years old, but hardly anyone pretends to understand the long-term effect of cell phone use. That hasn't stopped manufacturers and cell phone companies from introducing models just for kids. In Europe, available models have included the Foony, the Buddy Bear, and the i-kids phone. Even when the phones are off, their location is traceable. Costs are kept in check by letting parents pre-program allowable numbers so kids can't go calling halfway around the world. You can also determine in which narrow geographical "zone" your child is allowed to roam free; if he leaves the area, you'll receive an instant text message.

Automation tips for baby managers

Rapidly advancing technologies, combined with ballooning parental anxieties, ensure that various kinds of automated child warning systems will reach the market. Some children's advocates see this as a worrisome trend. Frank Furedi, a British sociology professor who authored the book *Paranoid Parenting: Why Ignoring the Experts May be Best For Your Child,* tells parents to stop obsessing about children's safety. "Sure, kids are vulnerable," he says, "but they're also resourceful and strong." Ironically, Furedi points out, banning risks creates all kinds of new dangers, because a cocooning parenting style tends to stunt a child's development. Then again, given the title of his book, he probably won't take offense if he's one of the experts you choose to ignore!

Profit & loss

11

Profit & loss

Investment

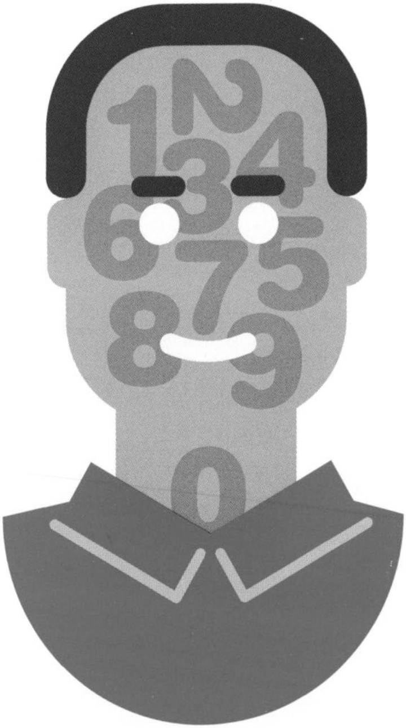

The launch and development of your product will require a substantial long-term investment in money, time, and attention. The yield, however, is necessarily a big unknown. In this chapter, we give you some insights into your product's profit potential, and in methods of planning that may help you arrive at the intended results.

Financial planning

"A child costs the equivalent of a Porsche," as they say (a bit unromantically) in Germany. Until he leaves the parental nest at (let's assume) age 18, your child will set you back more than $170,000 (or almost double that sum if you figure compound interest). With a bag of money like that, any Porsche dealer would be glad to show you his top-of-the-line models. Then again, as another saying goes, life is all about making choices. One small consolation is that the cost of additional children isn't strictly cumulative – the more children you have, the cheaper it is per child. In a two-parent household in the middle-income group, the estimated annual expense on a child age 0-2 with no siblings is around $14,000; for a baby and a 16-year-old teenager, it's $23,000; and for a baby, a 13-year-old and a 16-year-old, $27,000. So, while you're at it…

Budgeting

The biggest mistake you can make is assuming that the costs of having a child will only begin to escalate as it gets older. Usually, it's quite the contrary. Your baby may be satisfied with a rattle and won't yet make your brain explode with persistent demands for the latest cell phone, but the truth is, you're facing some hefty one-time startup costs, as well as potentially budget-wrecking expenses like babysitters and daycare. On top of that, your wife may cut back on her work hours. How much your baby is really going to cost you isn't an easy question. In fact, calculating the cost of children has become a science of sorts, not only for couples with genetic ambitions, but also for courts considering child support rules, and for governments distributing payments to support parents. Economists have agreed to disagree on this topic. For instance: should only real out-of-pocket costs be taken into account? Should college tuition or saving for a medical emergency be included? And should a lower standard of living also be weighed on the balance sheet? Let's say you and your wife love the good life. Every month you spend a significant amount on eating out. But since the baby came, you're happy when you get to eat out once every 3 months. It may not even be the money that's at issue, but now you're short on time, sleep, and you can rarely book a good babysitter – to name just a few obstacles. The arrival of the baby changed – lowered if you will – your standard of living. Should this "loss" be added to the costs of the child?

Price tag

To keep things simple, I leave this question to you. On the matter of what you really need to get by to meet basic needs, research by the Economic Policy Institute in Washington provided an answer. According to this think-tank, on average, an American family with two parents and two children requires an income of $48,778 to pay for the family budget. Obviously, there are big geographical differences. If you live in a rural area you won't need more than $35,733, whereas in a major urban area like Long Island, New York, your family has a price tag of $71,913. Some other points to consider: older children cost more in rural areas. Boys cost more than girls. Infants cost more in the city.

Your budget

This table should give you an idea of what you'll be facing in terms of monthly expenditures. The pages that follow supply more details about each individual expense.

	Income	Expenses	
Salary	....	....	Housing
Tax breaks	....	....	Phone
Deductibles	....	....	Insurance
Other government aid	....	....	Education
		....	Childcare
		....	Babysitters
		....	Contrib./subscriptions
		....	Transportation
		....	Hardware
		....	Software
		....	Medical expenses
		....	Recreational activities
		....	Personal care/hygiene
		....	Allowance
		....	Food
		....	Clothing
Total	....	....	

Expenditures

What are the minimum costs you're likely to face the first year?

Housing

Are you a renter? Then figure your actual rent, without utilities. Do you own your home? Calculate your net housing costs by subtracting your mortgage deductible from your mortgage payments. One half of the floor space of a house or apartment is typically used for communal purposes (kitchen, living space, hallways, etc.): therefore, divide your housing costs by two. Then divide that amount by the total number of rooms in your house, and multiply the result by the number of rooms that your child (or children) will occupy. Now you know by how much your housing expenses will go up. Once the baby arrives, your other housing expenditures, such as gas, heating oil, water, and electricity, are likely to go up by some 10 per cent.

Telephone

If you're on a calling plan that includes copious 'free" minutes, there might be no effect after the baby arrives. But if you pay by the call, reckon that the family addition will result in telephone bills that are about 25 per cent higher than usual. That's because you'll see increased calls to and from family members, healthcare providers, babysitters, and so on.

Insurance

Your insurance premiums will probably rise the month after your child is born. Ask your insurer how much.

Childcare

Childcare exists in many forms, with many different price tags. Actual costs depend mainly on where you live (region, city, or small town), on the quality of the daycare center, and on the hours you require. The full-time daycare rate (eight hours a day, five days a week) can vary from $350 to $1,400 a month. The average rate is around $600. Boston and New York are on the highest end, with rates well over $ 1,000; in San Antonio (Texas) you're all set for $350. In the U.K., the typical cost for a full-time nursery place for a child under two is $900. Additionally, you could be charged for diapers, snacks and meals, educational programs, laundry, or live webcam viewing (monitoring your kid online on the daycare center's website). Check the daycare arrangements your employer might have worked out for you such as a discount with a "preferred supplier" or a flexible spending account that allows employees to put aside money before taxes to pay for dependent care expenses. Most countries,

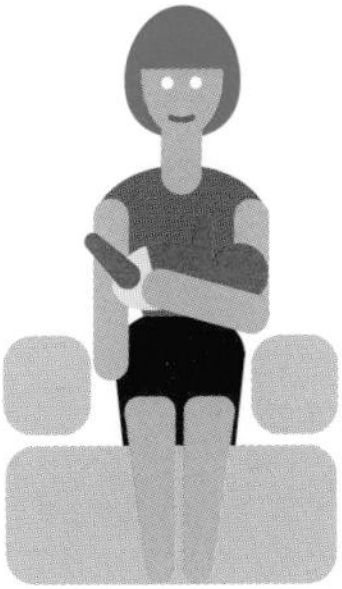

including the U.S., give you a tax credit for qualifying childcare expenses. How much you get back depends on your gross income. Apply in time or you might find the office window closed for the (fiscal) year – as I did.

Babysitter

In the U.S., the teenager who takes care of your child while you're enjoying an evening out is happy with $6 an hour. Again, rates depend on your location. In New York City, expect to pay at least $10 per hour; in rural areas $4 will do. Don't be too thrifty though: experience and reliability deserve something extra. A trustworthy babysitter allows you to regain some freedom. Need help at fixing a rate? **New-york-babysitters.com** offers a "baby sitter rate calculator", also useful if you don't reside in Manhattan.

Transportation

Auto: Every mile you drive for or with your child will set you back 40 to 60 cents, depending on the car you drive, your insurance rate, and your gas mileage. As for public transportation, most transportation companies let young children ride free. Inquire ahead. Most airlines don't charge for children under 2 as long as the child is seated on a parent or guardian's lap.

Hardware

You'll have to stock up on baby furniture, strollers, car seats, etc. Try to budget some money to decorate the nursery.

Software

This category combines what you spend on toys, books, and (later) on junior's sports and hobbies.

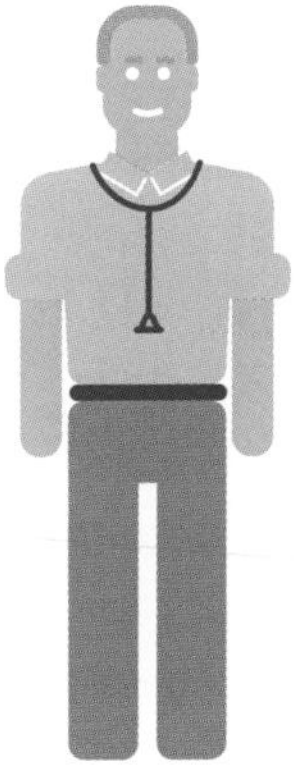

Medical costs

This category comprises all medical expenses not covered by your insurance company.

Recreation

Calculate what it costs to take your offspring to an amusement park, a zoo, and other recreational locations.

Personal care and hygiene

Lotions, creams, shampoos, soap, wet wipes – it all adds up. It'll take maybe $100-$125 to stock up on these materials, and after that you can maintain the supply for another $10–$12 a month, not including diapers. Diapers are a big expense. If you choose disposable ones, your child will go through about 4,500 of them before he is toilet-trained. Total costs: $2,300. Cotton diapers tend to be 25–50 per cent cheaper overall. If you happen to live in Seattle or the Dutch university town of Leyden, you can save even more. Considering that each child's disposables cost roughly $400 in municipal waste expenses, the local authorities have been providing parents with coupons worth up to $50 to $100 to purchase cloth diapers. It's an example that's being followed by many municipalities in Europe.

Allowance

Postpone the explanation of this word as long as possible. But when your child is about 6 years old, it's probably time to start giving him some weekly pocket money. There might be no need to put the allowance into your budget under its own category, though; whatever your child buys for himself is something you won't be called upon to buy *for* him.

Food

Your producer's intake will change during and after the assembly, and your product will need fuel, too. Roughly, it breaks down like this:

- Extra food for the mother during pregnancy: 30 cents a day
- Extra food for the mother during the breastfeeding period: about a dollar a day
- Food for an infant, up to one year old: $2–$3 a day
- Food for children aged one to three: $3–$4 a day

For formula, count on spending between $1,000–$2,300 during the first year – depending on whether you use powder or ready-to-pour liquids. Put aside at least $40 a week for infant formula. If your family consists of 2 parents with 2 or more children, the food costs per child decrease by about 12 per cent.

Clothing

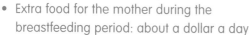

Coats, shoes, shirts, pants, pajamas: you're looking at buying your child an entire wardrobe – many times over, in fact, because he'll grow out of everything pretty quickly. You can make do with an initial

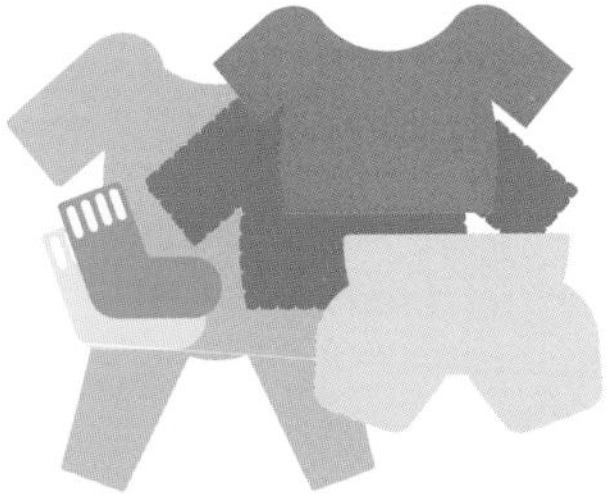

investment of $200–$300; after that, you'll probably need to spend $50–$60 a month.

Income

Looking for ways to offset the expenses? It's possible that Junior could indirectly make a little bit of money through tax breaks you'll receive. You may incur child-related deductible expenses, and receive financial aid from your government. Belgian dad Serge Régnier gives an inspiring example: he makes a living just out of being a father. With 31 children (from 3 different wives) to his name, this European fatherhood record-holder receives 6,700 dollars in child allowance per month. "Why should I work?" the Wallonian superdad asks. "There's enough work at home as it is!".

Time planning

Who is the ideal dad?

Ever since I started the father-centric website **www.ikvader.nl** in 2000, I've been a regular guest on talk shows and in the press, where I'm often asked what the "ideal father" looks like. One of the talk shows planned a broadcast on the theme "To mother, or to pursue a career?" These words had literally been created in neon, the sign illuminating a table to which 4 fathers had been invited for a public debate. When my turn came, I pointed out that the very way the theme had been worded was rather typical. The verb "to mother" has a clear, widely recognized definition – but "to father" (in English) means only a single act of procreation, and any other connotations are incidental or confusing.

It used to be crystal clear. For centuries, a father was counted on for 3 things: conceiving offspring, being the breadwinner, and exercising his paternal authority. Those 3 pillars of fatherhood are crumbling. Women are a lot more independent in many ways, including sexually and economically. In the West, they are no longer compatible with the kind of man who bangs his fists on the table to underscore his patriarchal power. These days, if a woman wants to get pregnant, you're hardly her only option. Gender roles are constantly being redefined; it's pointless to look back at what once was, and it's equally pointless to try to divine what the future holds. We'll just have to muddle through the here and now. So what does it mean to be a dad these days? Is it being "mother's big helper"? In order to be a responsible dad, are you supposed to tell your boss that you want a 32-hour work week?

Exit *pater familias*

You might not think it judging by the sharp debates over gender roles and parenting, but for hundreds upon hundreds of years, men and women shared an equitable consensus about raising their kids: they simply did it together. From the Batavians and the Romans until a century and a half ago, European dads played a little-changing role: they were the bearers of authority, the breadwinners, the protectors – and most of all, they were home. The watershed moment in the history of fatherhood was the Industrial Revolution. Until about

1850 there was no meaningful separation between home life and work. Household and place of business were a single unit. The vast majority of men worked the land around their homes, or had a home-based trade such as blacksmith or tailor. The second half of the 19th century brought a series of inventions and innovations: new materials like steel, new sources of energy like steam, coal, petroleum and electrical power, and new methods of transportation and communication such as powerful trains, steam-driven ships, the telegraph, and the radio. Those novelties were quickly refined and adopted, unleashing tectonic shifts in technology, the economy, and the overall culture. To apply the new technologies efficiently and on a grand scale, labor had to be organized differently. Work life and home life, once inseparably intertwined, were torn asunder – fathers left for long workdays in factories and offices. "The most prominent consequence that modernization has had on family life is no doubt the fact that fathers and other breadwinners were no longer physically present in the home all day," wrote the English family historian Peter Laslett. "The constant presence of fathers must have had a huge influence on families and households prior to the Industrial Revolution." The changeover presented many challenges. A British colleague of Laslett's, Adriennne Burgess, points out that the first generations of factory workers drove their bosses up the wall by taking breaks willy-nilly, and by staying at home for family gatherings deemed more important than the demands of work. Vacations? Sick days? Personal days? Unheard of. But over time, men became obedient office and factory slaves, and eventually reached the point where they believed that their jobs and careers were what truly mattered in life. After 20 centuries during which he'd been there for his children as a quasi-permanent educator, guide, and companion, man's home become the domain of the womenfolk.

As motherhood became a lofty, heavily idealized pursuit, men saw their domestic roles decline into irrelevance. Many of the things that they'd traditionally been tasked with were taken up by wives and schools. The erstwhile *pater familias* had turned into a *homo laboriosus* and, for short bursts only, a *homo ludens*: coming home after a day of back-breaking work, he'd briefly play with the kids.

37.7 seconds

The legacy of the Industrial Revolution is still with us today. Until about the mid-1970s, men took little part in the daily care of their young children. How little is hardly known. In 1971 two Boston psychologists, Freda Rebelsky and Cheryl Hanks, undertook a now-notorious attempt to discover "the truth" about "the new father", a term that was already being thrown around back then. The researchers attached voice-activated microphones to babies' clothes and recorded the length of time that child and father spent making noises to each other. This was done for 24 hours once a fortnight for the first 3 months of the child's life. The psychologists found that "fathers speak an average of 37.7 seconds a day to their 0–3 month-old-infants". The fact that Rebelsky and Hanks had only studied the vocalizations of a non-representative group of, all told, 19 fathers, did not dissuade them from offering their report to an authoritative scientific magazine. The article in *Child Development* was quoted out of context by newspapers worldwide, and some feminists eagerly used the study to substantiate their belief that men don't really care about kids.

3.5 hours

True, our predecessors weren't exactly overdoing it. A 1976 study reported that fathers took care of their children for about an hour each week, spending 45 minutes interacting with their offspring. Between 1987 and 1992, Australian dads have chosen to spend 2 more hours with their kids every week than they used to. Irrefutably, fathers are stepping up to the plate, no longer waiting until their children are 5 or 6 years old before getting involved. In Canada, the number of fathers reporting daily participation in childcare rose from 57 per cent in 1986 to 73 per cent in 2005. (90 per cent of mothers reported daily participation in both 1986 and 2005).

Dutch men, too, are becoming more involved. Between 1980 and 1995 their share of "unpaid labor" – a term that comprises both domestic and childcare tasks – went from 29 to 36 per cent. In the months before birth, you could even call Dutch men hyperactive. More than 83 per cent are busy preparing the nursery, 67 per cent accompany their wives during visits to the midwife or obstetrician, 66 per cent go shopping for a stroller, and a respectable 18 per cent take part in a course preparing for the delivery and beyond. While much has changed, much has remained the same. Although more women work today than ever before, after the baby is born the picture changes. In the U.S., the average wife does 31 hours of housework a week while the average husband does 14. If you break out couples in which wives stay at home and men are the sole breadwinners, the number of hours goes up for women, to 38 hours of housework a week, and somewhat down for men, to 12. When both partners have full-time paying jobs, the wife does 28 hours of housework and the husband 16. California sociologist Arlie Hochschild coined the phrase "the Second Shift" to describe the extra load of unpaid work women in dual-career households take upon themselves.

Lip service

It's a catchy phrase that does deserve some nuance. For example, fully-employed fathers tend to work longer hours than equally employed mothers. Like it or not, men earn more. So when the household requires extra money for the baby, men put in more hours – probably an echo of the old instinct to drag fresh meat to the cave. Interestingly, in the Netherlands, fathers of young children are the hardest workers. Compared to fathers of older children (14 and over), or even single or cohabiting men without kids, a young father spends far more hours earning an income. Just 10 per cent of them work fewer hours after they become a father. Moreover, what's the definition of housework in "the Second Shift"? Is it cooking, cleaning, ironing, dressing and feeding the kids, washing, and shopping? Or are car repairs, financial planning, doing homework with the kids, and building the new kitchen also included? Activities seen as typically male are usually left out of these gloomy reports. And it's also simply a matter of preference. Take a recent study on how parental-leave policies and gender role attitudes influence childcare responsibilities among male and female college professors. It concluded that even these highly ambitious women "simply like childcare more than men and are reluctant to cede many childcare duties to their husbands." Most women might encourage paternal involvement but can be critical about what they perceive as a lack of skill in their husbands' style of caring. Taking care of the children is not a task which they'd be happy to delegate to their husbands or partners. An American poll indicates that 60 to 80 per cent of all mothers do not wish fathers to participate more actively in raising children. Dutch mothers tend to be a bit more flexible, but legions of them still claim the right to act as the primary caregiver on the basis that, after all, they gave birth to the child.

I wish I could but I can't

Men would like this to be different – at least, that's what they say. In a 2002 poll by the Netherlands Institute of Care and Wellbeing, two-thirds of all men said they wanted to lavish more time on their children – and that they wouldn't mind spending more quality time with the dishes and the vacuum cleaner, either. But there were good reasons, they explained, why such wishes were just not realistic. Some 63 per cent declared that they'd perform more housework and childcare duties if only their job demands allowed it; 59 per cent if it were financially possible; and 25 per cent if it didn't badly affect hobbies and sports. More than half of the respondents opined that they wouldn't be able to improve upon their wives' care anyway – the mother, they said, was the more natural caregiver.

Some mothers complain about the male "I wish I could but I can't" mindset. Yet, at the same time, taking care of the children is not a task which they'd be happy to delegate to their husbands or partners, no matter how much they say they do.

I wish I could and I will

Let's assume for a few moments that all the obstacles have vanished. What would the ideal dad look like?

- **He's a partial breadwinner**
  A good job as a vehicle for self-worth and as the main source of money is still a primary motive, but he realizes that his paternal duties extend way beyond merely generating an income.

- **He's involved**
  He spends quality time with his kids: reading to them, playing with them, and helping them with personal problems and with homework. He is present physically and mentally, and he is approachable.
- **He shares responsibility**
  Father and mother both ensure their offspring's emotional balance, physical health, and they supply financial stability.
- **He's consistent**
  His behavior is the epitome of reliability. He realizes that children may learn more from what he does than from what he says.
- **He's caring**
  He is capable of offering security, and of giving (and receiving) affection, encouragement, and consolation.
- **He dispenses discipline**
  He knows how to nip unacceptable behavior in the bud – not with threats or violence, but drawing on the strong bonds that develop between him and his children.

Time management!

Don't sell yourself short while trying to play the "ideal dad". Spend as much time with your family as is necessary for your wellbeing and theirs. Strive for a satisfactory balance: your happiness is a terrifically positive and appealing example. Not enough time? Here are 6 time-management tips:

1. Plan your work and family to-dos. Sit down with your spouse and draw up a schedule dividing domestic and childcare tasks. Keep a special calendar for appointments that involve both of you, and go over the upcoming events at least once a week.
2. Do everything that must be done soon as soon as possible. Don't postpone unpleasant but necessary tasks.

3. Finish one job at a time. Then take a break and start on the next.
4. Eliminate external timewasters. Do you get unexpected phone calls, e-mails, or visitors? They can wait!
5. Never say yes if you mean no.
6. It won't hurt you to switch off your cell phone a little more frequently.

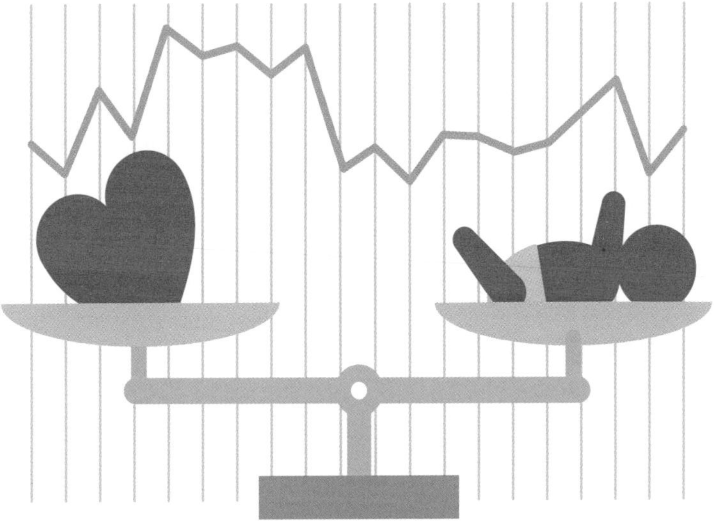

Yield

Analysts, trend watchers and futurologists are powerless. Even fortune tellers can't give you a reliable estimate of future profits in the happiness department!

How much chance of happiness?

That a child ought to reward your investment with happiness is a recent notion. Your ancestors produced far more children and saw a good percentage of them perish due to contagious diseases, poor food, and questionable hygiene. The surviving children were first and foremost a kind of guaranteed pension: with whatever they could contribute to the family's bottom line, the kids were insurance against bad times, and a source of care when the parents become too old and frail to work. These days, children are tasked with contributing to their parents' emotional wellbeing. How likely are they to succeed?

Blessed with kids

As long as the child is healthy and the mother recovers without lasting complications, your path to happiness is virtually guaranteed. Or anyway, that seems to be the prevailing sentiment. Polls show that a large majority of men and women find that a marriage without kids is incomplete; it isn't money but the blessings associated with producing offspring that provide happiness. Still, researchers say the picture is more complicated than that.

What is happiness?

That was a matter long left for philosophers and clergy to ponder. For thousands of years they've been pontificating on this basic question. But in the 1960s, social scientists began grappling with the same issue. Sociologist Ruut Veenhoven, of the Erasmus University in Rotterdam, has gathered all scientific answers into his World Database of Happiness. Veenhoven defines happiness as "the degree to which an individual judges the overall quality of his life as positive". Such a judgment is influenced by internal and external factors. An internal factor is, for instance, the "life ability" of an individual (health, skills, and the capacity to make proper choices and to experience enjoyment). Of course, Veenhoven and his fellow happiness researchers have also looked at the role that children play in our overall contentment. They looked at existing research projects that sought to reveal how having children, or not having children, impacts on marital contentment. Thousands of couples were interviewed to arrive at these combined results. The conclusion? Having kids is hardly a sure-fire path to overall euphoria.

Crisis

Researchers report a rise in the happiness curve (the so-called honeymoon high) during the first phase of marriage, with a peak during the first pregnancy. After the birth, the curve goes down as a result of "parental crisis". Partly due to financial pressures, changing sex lives, and an underlying discontent about the new parental roles, men and women enter a phase that is decidedly less rosy. "Even the best children with the most conventional parents exert wear and tear on marriage relations," wrote one researcher. A second child further flattens the curve. However, as soon as the children become substantially independent (when they start going to school), the relationship typically flourishes again. Studies also show that a childless marriage is often far from emotionally barren. Couples who are childless by choice do not appear to experience a diminished sense of happiness or wellbeing. Older married people without children report feeling better than their demographic brethren who do have offspring.

Net results

Whether your children will bring you the intended "happiness yield" depends on a number of factors:

- **Wanted or not?** – Couples who have more children than they bargained for report being less happy.
- **Type of relationship** – Couples with a "closed" relationship characterized by a strong emotional interdependence see their satisfaction with their marriage decrease after kids enter the picture. Couples who enjoyed a freer relationship BC (before

children), and who had a variety of non-domestic interests, experience more satisfaction after having children.

- **Financial position** – Wealthy couples are three times more dissatisfied about their marriage after having kids than couples from blue-collar and middle-class families.

More info: The World Database of Happiness is at **www.worlddatabaseofhappiness.eur.nl.**

Write-offs

Hours of sleep

Lack of sleep is a formidable enemy. During the first months, the baby will need to be fed every 2–3 hours, even at night. That's not conducive to perfect well-being, to put it mildly. Sleep researchers say that a lack of shut-eye produces very similar effects to those induced by drinking a large amount of alcohol. Your brain's and muscles' response time goes down by half, and your ability to concentrate and stay mentally alert also takes a beating. Besides, not getting enough sleep is likely to make you pack on a few pounds. It makes your insulin levels fluctuate, which results in your body craving candy and other junk food. There are 2 viable solutions:

- **Sleep separately** – Especially during the first weeks and months, you'll be bound to frequently startle awake with worry. Is junior still breathing? What was that odd sound emanating from the crib? Do yourself a favor: wear earplugs and/or go crash in a different room, away from your child and your producer. You'll be more use to her the next day that way.

- **Your child sleeps through the night** – The happy day when your child sleeps like a log from evening till morning often doesn't arrive for a year, but some children sleep through the night at the ripe old age of 3 months.

Your past life

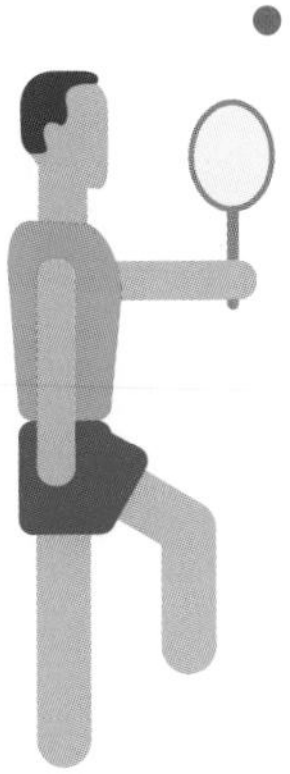

Grab a beer with Bob? Visit the game with Gary? Better begin practicing your new mantra: "Sorry, guys, I wish I could but you know how it is." Your new status robs you of a lot of your spare time. If you know what's good for you, stop looking back at the leisure paradise you left behind. Your past life is now irrelevant. What counts is exploring the possibilities in your new one. Buy a portable futon and take your baby to parties.

Your old sex life

Becoming a father is surely a terrific gift, but it isn't without downsides. You could be an exception to the rule, but most couples have to face the music: their sex life together will never return to the fire, intensity, and frequency that once characterized it. The four big obstacles are lack of sleep, time pressures, hormonal changes, and the physical post-pregnancy effects for your partner. Polls indicate that 50 per cent of mothers admit that they don't much feel like having sex in the first year after the baby arrives. One common reason is that they throw themselves into motherhood with such abandon that their desire for intimacy and physical bonding is largely satisfied by the child. Men have the tendency to lose themselves in their jobs. No worries. The experts believe that sexual pleasure is still well attainable, but the return of intimacy requires some work. The loving relationship that produced your baby shouldn't become a series of chores and obligations. Set aside one night a week in that joint calendar. Take her out, seduce her, and keep discovering why you chose her as the perfect mate for this adventure to begin with.

Bonuses

For your child

It took ages before reliable research data came out about the effects that fathers have on the development of their children. One obstacle was Sigmund Freud, whose influential theory about early child development and parental impact identified mothers as the crucial factor. Another barrier was put in place by the British psychiatrist John Bowlby. This author of *Attachment Theory* posited that children, especially during their critical phases as babies and toddlers, cannot flourish without motherly love. "Long periods of missing a mother's care can have dramatic effects on a young child's character, and these effects may

persist for the rest of his life." Bowlby expertly sold that notion in the advice he gave to the World Health Organization and other groups. Later in his career, he acknowledged that other caregivers can play a healthy role in a child's life, but he never retracted his statements on the virtues and preeminence of motherhood. To Bowlby, fathers were bit players at best. He had lots of company in that belief. The role of fathers has been virtually ignored in decade after decade of studies purporting to chart "parental" influence. Time after time, report titles referred to the significance or the opinions of parents; the actual content would subsequently reveal that the researchers had solicited only the input of mothers. Thus was born the "scientifically rooted" impression that the desired involvement of fathers in raising kids was pretty much limited to their being good providers. It took a long time for this attitude to change. In 1995, U.S. President Bill Clinton decreed that mothers and fathers should have equal "weight" in research and policy initiatives concerning the raising and educating of children. Five years later, for the first time, men were finally included in the prominent National Survey of Family Growth. In the Netherlands, it was especially Louis Tavecchio, a child development professor at the University of Amsterdam, who agitated against fathers being carelessly excluded from parenting studies. In a 2002 lecture, he challenged his audience to refuse research requests "in which fathers are ignored without rhyme or reason, or, worse yet, in which the focus is purportedly on parents even though only mothers are mentioned as useful research subjects. Please don't hesitate to immediately return all such research proposals to sender." Tavecchio publicly found fault with the fact that "much of our acquired knowledge about raising children is based on the mother's psychology and pedagogy"; and he severely criticized several big, long-running studies into education and childcare in which fathers were evidently seen as vaguely irrelevant breadwinners cum part-time babysitters. He called this an "expensive, systematic shortcoming," especially in light of more up-to-date studies revealing that fathers and mothers have clear differences in how they think about education and child-rearing, and that the development of the child can be better predicted with data gleaned from the fathers.

In recent years, social scientists and researchers have been taking fathers far more seriously. Though this catch-up effort results in more than 700 papers on men's family roles being published in academic journals worldwide each year, there are still many gaps to be filled. Here are some conclusions from studies that follow children who grow up with and without a dad:

Children who grow up without a father:

- have a higher rate of failing in school, and a higher chance of becoming dropouts;
- have a higher incidence of behavioral problems;
- have more problems with drugs and alcohol;
- often overcompensate when it comes to displaying "male" behavior (boys) – a desire to prove their manliness that can result in theft and/or violence.

Children with involved fathers:

(fathers who perform 40 per cent or more of childcare)

- have better motor skills;
- are less traditional in how they think about gender roles;
- are more independent, self-assured, compassionate, and mentally stable;
- have fewer problems going through puberty.

The differences can be explained by the ways in which a father's interactions with his children is distinct from the mother's, and by the role model that fathers offer.

For your partner

Are you working harder than ever before? That's understandable. Expenses have gone up, your spouse might work fewer hours after having given birth, you may find yourself in a career upswing. But this is hardly the time to neglect the home front. That goes double if your wife has the common inclination to become the Perfect Mom. More and more women have come to experience a job as an obstacle to flawless motherhood. Large numbers of women burn out young. If you do your part of the housework, or at least do enough so that she feels supported, you're in for some pleasant surprises. A survey conducted by fatherhood writer Neil Chethik suggests that maneuvering the vacuum cleaner now and then serves as a potent aphrodisiac. "The happier a wife is with her husband's participation in housework, the more sex she has with him," Chethik claims. His findings have been broadly confirmed by social research. An in-depth 2007 study concluded that there is a "positive and linear relationship" between men's involvement with the kids and the satisfaction that couples derive from their marriage. In other words: if necessary, force your wife to delegate some tasks to you. Good for her, good for your relationship.

For you

Asked what adds the most quality to their lives, people usually mention their personal relationships (their feelings about their children, their spouse, their marriage) before they enumerate financial issues (income, standard of living, accumulated wealth). Above a certain level, a higher income no longer contributes to happiness. And above a certain age, you're long past the "happiness slump" that having young kids induced way back when. In the U.S., several studies reveal worlds about the long-term effects of fatherhood. Thousands of men were scrutinized over the course of their lives, and some researchers are even following the offspring of these subjects. The following conclusions can be drawn:

- Fatherhood increases a man's self-knowledge and his readiness and ability to empathize.
- Men who experience their father role as something positive, more often volunteer for leadership positions in their communities and professions.
- Fatherhood boosts a man's aptitude for expressing his feelings.
- The more fathers are involved in raising their children, the higher the chance that they'll experience long-term contentment in their marriages.

Crucial ability

What makes a life worth living? Put differently, what should you do to look back on your life when you're elderly, and feel that it was a success? Many answers are possible, but two keep pushing themselves to the foreground: the ability to form and maintain intimate relationships, and the ability to be generative. That word comprises all the efforts and activities that contribute to the development of a new generation of people. There are many ways to develop that ability: by being creative and making art, by passing on knowledge and experience to others, by conceiving and raising kids. In order to be generative, becoming a father is not a necessity. Rather, it is an opportunity, a chance, a challenge that, if you choose to accept it, will have a long and lasting impact on your life.

Bibliography

Allison, C., "Disposable diapers, potential health hazards?", Sacramento Parent Magazine, March 2000

Anderson, R.C., Acute Respiratory Effects of Diaper Emissions, Archives of Environmental Health 54, October 1999

Australian Institute of Family Studies, "A Guide to Calculating the Costs of Children", 2000

Badinter, E., The myth of motherhood. An historical view of the maternal instinct. London, 1981

Baker, R., Oram, E., Baby Wars: the dynamics of family conflict, London, 1998

Belkin, L. Orgasms During Childbirth? New York Times, December 11, 2008

Benthem van-Jutting, W., Onderzoek naar het vaderschap. Het vaderschap als ethisch en godsdienstig vraagstuk. Van Loghum Slaterus, Arnhem, 1959

Blum, D., Love at Goon Park: Harry Harlow and the Science of Affection, Perseus Publishing, Cambridge, 2002

Borgenicht, L., Borgenicht, J., The Baby Owner's Manual, Quick Books, Philadelphia, 2003

Boswell, J., The Kindness of Strangers: The abandonment of children in Western Europe from late antiquity to the renaissance, University of Chicago Press, 1998

Bowlby, J., "The nature of a child's tie to his mother", International Journal of Psychoanalysis, 1958

Burgess, A., Fatherhood Reclaimed. The Making of the Modern Father, London, 1997

Busse, T., Seeaydarian, L., "First names and popularity in grade school children", Psychology in the Schools, 2006

Breeuwsma, G., De constructie van de levensloop. Boom, Amsterdam/Meppel, 1994

Carlson, S.E., Werkman, S.H., J.M. Peeples, W.M. Wilson, "Long-chain fatty acids and early visual and cognitive development of preterm infants", European Journal of Clinical Nutrition, 1994

Chethik, N. HusbandSpeak Survey, University of Kentucky Survey Research Center, 2004

Clare, A., On Men, Random House U.K., London, 1998

Cohen, P. "Daddy Dearest: Do You Really Matter? Everyone Agrees You Do, but So Far No One Has Established Why", New York Times, July 7, 1998

Cunningham, H., Children and Childhood in Western Society since 1500, Addison-Wesley, London, 1995

De Villiers & The Villiers, Language acquisition, Harvard University Press, Cambridge, 1978

Dietz, W.H., "Breastfeeding may help prevent childhood overweight", Journal of the American Medical Association, 2001

Douglas, S., Michaels, M., The Mommy Myth. The Idealization of Motherhood and How It Has Undermined Women, Simon & Schuster, New York, 2004

Driessen, G. "The Feminization of Primary Education: Effects of Teachers' Sex on Pupil

Achievement, Attitudes and Behaviour', International Review of Education, 2006
Erikson, E., Identity and the Life Cycle, London, 1980
Farrisi, T., Diaper Changes (Rev. ed.), Homekeepers Publishing, Pennsylvania, 1999
Fieldeldij Dop, J. en P., Dat leuke eerste jaar, Agon Amsterdam, 1994
Freud, S., Drei Abhandlungen zur Sexualtheorie. Franz Deuticke, Leipzig/Vienna, 1905
Furedi, F., Paranoid Parenting: Why Ignoring the Experts May Be Best for Your Child, Chicago Review Press, Chicago, 2002
Gerritsen, W.J., "PCB's en dioxinen hebben negatieve effecten", Voeding Nu, The Hague, 1999
Gerstein, H.C., "Cow's milk exposure and type I diabetes mellitus", Diabetes Care, 1994 Gezondheidsraad: Voedingsnormen; energie, eiwitten, vetten en verteerbare koolhydraten, The Hague, 2001
Gezondheidsraad: Voedingsnormen; calcium, vitamine D, thiamine, riboflavine, niacine, pantotheenzuur en biotine, The Hague, 2000
Hamosh, M., "Breastfeeding and the working mother: effect of time and temperature of short term storage on proteolysis, lipolysis and bacterial growth in milk", Pediatrics, 1996
Hanson, S.M.H., Bozett, F.W., Dimensions of Fatherhood, Sage Publications, Thousand Oaks, 1985
Harmsen, H.J.M., Wildeboer-Veloo, A.C.M., G.C. Raangs, A.A. Wagendorp, N. Heath, D.H., "What meaning and effects does fatherhood have for the maturing of professional men?", Merrill-Palmer Quarterly, 1978
Healy, M., "Breast-Feeding Beyond Babyhood", Los Angeles Times, February 5, 2001
Heath, D.H., Heath, H.E., Fullfilling Lives: Paths to Maturity and Success, San Francisco 1991
Hewlett, B., Intimate Fathers: the nature and content of Aka Pygmy paternal infant care, Ann Arbor, Michigan, 1991
Hoffman, J. and Ravenara, Z. "Are Fathers Pulling Their Weight at Home?" Father Involvement Research Allicance, 2008
Huizinga, J., Homo Ludens, a study of the play element in culture, Maurice Temple Smith Ltd, London, 1970
IGZ-bulletin: Voeding van zuigelingen en peuters. Uitgangspunten voor de voedingadvisering voor kinderen van 0-4 jaar, IGZ/Voedingscentrum, The Hague, 1999
Itz, C., Mannen in beeld – hoe de overheid zorg aan de man kan brengen, Doctoral thesis. Bestuurskunde en Vrouwenstudies, University van Amsterdam, 2002
Jones, S., Martin, R., D. Pilbeam, S. Bunney, The Cambridge Encyclopedia of Human Evolution, Cambridge University Press, Cambridge, 1992
Kalmijn, M., De Graaf, P.M., "Gescheiden vaders en hun kinderen: een empirische analyse van voogdij en bezoekfrequentie", Bevolking en Gezin, 2000
Karjalainen, J., Martin, J.M., M. Knip, J. Ilonen, B.H. Robinson, E. Savilahti, "A bovine albumin peptide as a possible trigger of insulin-dependent diabetes mellitus", New England Journal of Medicine, 1992
Knijn, T., "Hij wil wel maar hij kan niet. Over zorgend vaderschap en mannelijke genderidentiteit", Psychologie & Maatschappij, 1990

Kostraba, J.N., Cruickshanks, K.J., J. Lawler-Heavner, L.F. Jobim, M.J. Rewers, E.C. Gay, "Early exposure to cow's milk and solid foods in infancy, genetic predisposition, and risk of IDDM", Diabetes, 1993

Kuntz, C., Lonnerdal, B., "Re-evaluation of the whey protein/casein ratio of human milk", Acta Paediatrica Scandinavica, 1992

Kunz, C., Rodriguez-Palmero, M., B. Koletzko, R. Jensen, "Nutritional and biochemical properties of human milk, part I: General aspects, proteins, and carbohydrates", Clinics in Perinatology, 1990

Landbank Consultancy, A review of Procter & Gamble's environmental balances for disposable and re-usable nappies, London, 1991

Lanting, C.I., Effects of perinatal PCB and dioxin exposure and early feeding mode on child development, Proefschrift RijksUniversity, Groningen, 1999

Leach, P., Your baby & child, Penguin books, London 1997

Lee, Chih-Yuan S., Doherty, William J. "Marital satisfaction and father involvement during the transition to parenthood", Men's Study Press, March, 2007

Lehrburger, C., "The disposable diaper myth, out of sight, out of mind', Whole Earth Review, 1988

Levine, J.A., Pittinsky, T.L., Working Fathers, New Strategies for Balancing Work and Family, Addison-Wesley, New York 1997

Lewin, T., 3 New Studies Assess Effects of Child Care, New York Times, November 1, 2005

Lewis, C. Lamb, M. Understanding fatherhood, A review of recent research. Joseph Rowntree Foundation, 2007

Lin, J.; Bernstein, J. "What we need to get by. A basic standard of living costs $48,778, and nearly a third of families fall short", EPI Briefing Paper #224, 2008

Lust, K.D., Brown, J.E., W. Thomas, "Maternal intake of cruciferous vegetables and other foods and colic symptoms in exclusively breast-fed infants", Journal of the American Dietetic Association, 1996

Malinowski, B., The Father in Primitive Psychology, Taylor & Francis Books, London, 1927

McConnell, J., "Joy of cloth diapering", Mothering, 1988

McLanahan, S., Sandefur, G., Growing up with a single parent: What hurts, what helps, Harvard University Press, Cambridge, 1994

Meyerhoff, Michael K., "Of Baseball and Babies: Are You Unconsciously Discouraging Father Involvement in Infant Care?", Young Children, May, 1994

Morris, D., Babywatching, 1991

Mothering staff, "The politics of diapers: a timeline of recovered history". Mothering Magazine, 2003

Ninio, A., Rinott, N., "Fathers' involvement in the care of their infants and their attribution of cognitive competence to infants", Child Development, 1988

Pardou, A., "Human milk banking: influence of storage processes and the bacterial contamination of some milk constituents", Biology of the neonate, 1994

Parker, K. Save the Males, why men matter, why women should care. Random House, New York, 2008

Patandin, S.,'Effects of environmental exposure to polychlorinated biphenyls and dioxins on growth and development in young children", Thesis Erasmus University, Rotterdam, 1999
Pessers, D., "Vaders doen er niet toe, kinderen zijn de dupe: de macht van de moeder is Grenzeloos", NRC/Handelsblad, December 20, 2004
Piaget, J., Some Aspects of Origins from Play and Development, W.W. Norton & Company, New York, 1972
Pollock, L.A., A lasting relationship. Parents and children over three centuries, Fourth Estate, London, 1987
Portegrijs, W., Boelens A., S. Keuzenkamp, Emancipatiemonitor 2002, SCP and CBS, The Hague, 2002
Porter, R., The Economics of Waste, RFF Press, 2002
Primomo, J., "The high environmental cost of disposable diapers", American Journal of Maternal/Child Nursing, 1990
Pruett K.D., Role of the father. Pediatrics, 1998
Rebelsky, F., Hanks, C., "Fathers' Verbal Interactions with Infants in the First Three Months of Life", Child Development, 1971
Remery, C., Schippers, J., "Arbeid-zorgarrangementen in organisaties: een analyse van werkgeversgedrag", Bevolking en Gezin 31, 2002
Roedholm, M., "Effect of father-infant postpartum contact in their interaction 3 months after birth", Early Human Development 5, 1981
Romain, N., Dandrifosse, G., F. Jeusette, P. Forget, "Polyamine concentration in rat milk and infant formula", Pediatric Research, 1992
Runzheimer International, "What Will Childcare Cost You?" Mobility Report, 2006
Sagasser, J., Schiet, M., Omgaan met je kind, Tirion publishers, Baarn, 2000
Shapiro, A., Lambert, J.D., "Longitudinal effects of the divorce on the quality of the father-child relationship and on father's psychological well-being", Journal of Marriage and the Family, 1999
Sheehy, G., Understanding Men's Passages. Discovering the new map of men's lives, Random House, New York, 1998
Tavecchio, L., Van Opvang naar Opvoeding. De emancipatie van een uniek opvoedingsmilieu, Vossiuspers UvA, Amsterdam, 2002
Timmerman, G.; Essen van, M., "The myth of the 'women peril'. A historical review of (inter) national studies into the relationship between feminisation and boys". Pedagogiek, 2004
TNO Preventie en Gezondheid, Peiling Melkvoeding van Zuigelingen 2001/ 2002 en het effect van certificering op de borstvoedingscijfers, December 2002
Twenge, J. M., Campbell, W. K., C. A. Foster, "Parenthood and marital satisfaction: A meta-analytic review", Journal of Marriage and the Family, 2003
Tormo, R., Potau, N., D. Infante, "Protein in infant formula; future aspects of development", Early Human Development, 1998
U.S. Department of Agriculture, Center for Nutrition Policy and Promotion. Expenditures on Children by Families. Miscellaneous Publication Number 1528-2007.

Veenhoven, R., Kiezen voor kinderen. Zijn kinderen goed voor het huwelijk?, Intermediair, Amsterdam/Van Gorcum, Assen, Amsterdam, 1977

WHO Working group on the growth reference protocol and the WHO Task Force on methods for the natural regulation of fertility, "Growth of healthy infants and the timing, type and frequency of complementary foods", American Journal of the clinical nutrician, 2002

Working Group on Cow's Milk Protein and Diabetes Mellitus of the American Academy of Pediatrics, "Infant feeding practices and their possible relationship to the etiology of diabetes mellitus", Pediatrics, 1994

Zander, J., "Zorgende vader bestaat niet in officiële teksten", Trouw, April 2000

Index